REVOLUTION FROM BELOW

Buddhist and Christian Movements for Justice in Asia

Four Case Studies from Thailand and Sri Lanka

Robert Bobilin
University of Hawaii

UNIVERSITY PRESS OF AMERICA

Lanham • New York • London

University Press of America,® Inc.

4720 Boston Way
Lanham, MD 20706

3 Henrietta Street
London WC2E 8LU England

Printed in the United States of America

British Cataloging in Publication Information Available

Library of Congress Cataloging-in-Publication Data

Bobilin, Robert, 1924–
Revolution from below : Buddhist and Christian movements for justice in Asia : four case studies from Thailand and Sri Lanka /Robert Bobilin.
p. cm. Bibliography: p.
1. Buddhism and social problems—Sri Lanka—Case studies.
2. Buddhism and social problems—Thailand—Case studies.
3. Christian Workers Fellowship (Sri Lanka)—Case studies.
4. Social justice—Case studies. I. Title.
HN40.B8B63 1988
294.3'378'095493—dc 19 88–14830 CIP
ISBN 0–8191–7037–2 (alk. paper)
ISBN 0–8191–7038–0 (pbk. : alk. paper)

All University Press of America books are produced on acid-free paper which exceeds the minimum standards set by the National Historical Publications and Records Commission.

To the memory of my father, Theodore C. Bobilin,
and my father-in-law, Frank S. Williams

Preface and Acknowledgements

My thesis is that contemporary religious reflection should expand to include socio-economic change. This book presents some examples of how Buddhists and Christians are working for social justice and an alternative economic order. In Asian history religion has been related to peasant rebellions, just kings, and scriptures presenting an economic ethic. As religious leaders become historically self-conscious they can choose the socio-ethical paradigms which may suit their own situation. During the sixties and the seventies there emerged a number of movements in South and Southeast Asia that responded to the problems of economic injustice and neo-colonialism. Leaders and others in these movements are re-reading their traditions in the light of the needs and goals of persons in present-day life. The purpose of this writing is to provide an outline of the socio-economic teaching, the role of founders and leaders, and the social action of four movements in Sri Lanka and Thailand.

Of particular interest is the Buddhist reflection that is integral to these groups. Although one movement is Christian, all demonstrate the impact of western and Christian influences on their societies. The movements have been chosen because they appeared to be good instances of "creative tension" with the social order. They are "engaged" in ways that show profound concern for the people and traditions of their cultures, but also for ethical goals that have become an integral part of their vision for the future of society. Social vision never comes easy. These movements have been involved in struggle and conflict. They have had to face the opposition of governments.

This study owes much to the encouragement, kindness, and patience of the leaders of the four movements that are the basis of this research. A.T. Ariyaratne, Anna and Jeffrey Abesekerya, Kingsley Perera, Sulak Sivaraksa, Dr. Seri Phongphit, and many others were immensely helpful. Very important was the collegial support of faculty and staff at Chulalongkorn University, particularly Professor Soomboon Suksaram and the Thai Studies Department. The Philosophy Department at Chiengmai University--particularly

Professor Siddhi Butr-Indr--was very gracious and resourceful. Payap College was very responsive to our needs and provided hospitality while we were in Chiengmai. To Rossana Tositrukul, my research assistant in Bangkok, my gratitude for her consistent support and endurance of long bus and train rides. In Sri Lanka I benefitted from the assistance of the late Lynn De Silva, the staff of the Marga Institute, and the University of Peredeniya. Many friends and faculty at the University of Peredeniya made my stay there most helpful. Professor R.A. Gunatilike was a great host and provided major encouragement for my work. Mr. H. Jayasena was very helpful as a research assistant in Colombo.

The Institute for Southeast Asian Studies in Singapore provided hospitality, library resources, and stimulating discussions with many staff members for a stay in the summer of 1983.

Major financial support came from the generous Maryknoll Fathers and Brothers through a Walsh-Price Fellowship. This grant provided resources for field work and travel that supplemented a sabbatical leave from the University of Hawaii.

To colleagues in the Department of Religion at the University of Hawaii, Professors Alfred Bloom and David Chappell and Sister Joan Chatfield many, many thanks for their consistent encouragement and collegial support. The faculty and staff of the Center for Asian and Pacific Studies provided many useful suggestions and key contacts for my work.

I have benefitted from many discussions with Bhikkhu Buddhatat, Father Tissa Balasuryia, Phra Rajavaramuni, David Kalupahana, and Donald Swearer.

My appreciation to Janet Honda for her intelligent typing and many revisions accomplished in the Department of Religion office.

Finally, to my wife who endured storms, theft, and many long field trips and yet provided stimulating companionship--my great appreciation.

Table of Contents

...And in those days all men and beasts
Shall surely be in mortal danger
For when the Monarch shall betray
The Ten Virtues of the Throne
Calamity will strike, the omens
Sixteen monstrous apparitions:
Moon, stars, earth, sky shall lose their course
Misfortune shall spread everywhere
Pitch-black the thundercloud shall blaze
With Kali's fatal conflagration
Strange signs shall be observed throughout
The land, the Chao Phraya River shall boil
Red as the heart's blood of a bird
Madness shall seize the Earth's wide breast
Yellow the colour of the leading sky.
The forest spirits race to haunt
The city, while to the forest flee
The city spirits seeking refuge ...
The enamel tie shall rise and float
The light gourd sink down to the depths.

Translated from a Thai poem of the seventeenth century by B. Anderson in _Bulletin of Concerned Asian Scholars_, Vol. 9, No. 3, July 1977

I

INTRODUCTION

Religion as Ideology and Utopia

Karl Mannheim has helped us to see that religion functions both as an ideology and as a utopia. It is ideological if it legitimates the existing social order, defends the dominant values, and enhances the authority of the dominant class; it is utopian if it reveals the ills of the social order, evokes criticism of the dominant groups, and releases energy for social change. Both Buddhism and Christianity operate at both levels--sometimes simultaneously. Religion probably never quite equals the ideological, yet it has provided a basis for ideology since ancient times.

Religion has been used both to defend and to break up feudalism in Asia and Europe. Francois Houtart has argued, for example, that right down to the end of the nineteenth century the entire feudal system of Sri Lanka was ideologically served by popular Buddhist teachings. And when religion in the form of missions intertwines with mercantilism and colonial expansion, it frequently sanctifies the nationalistic arrogance of the colonizing power.

But Dr. M. Palihawadana has suggested that a new utopian development--socialism in Sri Lanka--is inspired by the Buddhist vision on the one hand and the Marxist economic vision on the other. And Professor E. Sarkisyanz demonstrates how in Burma the ideal future envisaged in Buddhist scriptures reinforced U Nu's efforts toward egalitarianism and freedom from oppression.

Undoubtedly, one of the difficulties of dealing with this subject is due to the paradoxical nature of religion itself. Religion, however interpreted in different contexts, has both universal and particular dimensions. It must be particular, because its universal elements must be communicated; yet communication is not to human beings in general but to persons in specific times and places. In this sense, the history of every religion may be seen as a dialectical process in which the universalization of the particular and the particularization of the universal are intricately intertwined. Unfortunately, religion often legitimates the power structure.

Mannheim recognizes the significance of the "Utopian mentality" in religion, particularly in times of cultural crisis:

> In periods of rapid social change, there must be small groups that explore new cultural possibilities, and perform experiments in living for others. In this fashion they create new types of experiences which may later become the general pattern.[1]

It is with the thought of discerning movements with the "Utopian mentality" that I investigate Buddhist and Christian movements for social criticism and action in contemporary Thailand and Sri Lanka.

The Meaning of "utopia"

In common usage, utopia is often used in a derogatory sense to refer to unrealistic otherworldly dreams or some kind of ideal but static future state. Mannheim makes it clear that utopias in his use of the term characterize groups that embody socially transforming images in their own conduct. In this study we examine the interplay between social goals (or utopias) and social-historical experience in two countries. To use Ernst Bloch's expression, we are considering "concrete utopias" rather than abstract utopias. The relationship between an existing social order and a utopia is a dialectical one. Values in the utopian group or movement "become the explosive material for bursting the limits of the existing order."[2] It is difficult, of course, to determine what is genuinely transforming in the first stirrings of a new movement.

Related to the "concrete utopia" idea is Robert Bellah's concept of "creative tension". He suggests that most religions display a complex of social tendencies--fusion, disjunction, and creative tension--toward their world and culture. Religion may sanctify a given social-cultural order and provide little leverage to change it--an instance of Mannheim's Ideology. But in some instances, religious action consists of avoiding as much of the world as possible. A group that focuses on complex states of consciousness may have little direct impact on the social order, and other groups may be so alienated from social institutions and the decision-making process that disjuncture or withdrawal may occur. Creative tension exists when transcendent ideals are in tension with empirical reality, the world is seen as a meaningful place for religious action.[3]

It is important that a socioreligious movement be studied not only at the level of ideas or doctrines, since its teaching or its symbol system is only one aspect of its relation to the social situation. For example, the leadership training and discipline given to workingmen in the early Wesleyan movement in England became a leadership resource for the British Labour Party--although that was certainly not the intention of John Wesley. The Sangha--the Buddhist monkhood--in Burma became a vehicle for national unity under U Nu mainly because it reached across class and ethnic lines. The Sangha and the Temple provide models of detachment in South and Southeast Asian culture that may either provide broader ethical perspectives on social issues or allow social energy to be absorbed in pious ritual. The point is that, in addition to its religious teaching on ethical issues, the group's pattern of operation in a society and culture may have important consequences. The way a group is organized and functions may, in fact, serve as a transcendent norm for a society.

Of the movements we examine, two had their beginnings in the late 1950s, two in the 1970s. Perhaps these were periods of relative openness in Sri Lanka and Thailand. Barrington Moore informs us from his study of social and moral transformations that "social and cultural space within the prevailing order is prerequisite to the inception of such movements:

> A society with social and cultural space provides more or less protected enclaves within which dissatisfied or oppressed groups have some room to develop distinctive social arrangements, cultural traditions, and explanations of the world around them. Social and cultural space implies room to experiment with making the future.[4]

The early 1950s were a time of social ferment in Sri Lanka, which had just achieved independence from the British. In Thailand the student uprising of 1973 perhaps signaled a short period of greater openness in Thai society. New social movements or forms, as Gaetano Mosca points out, are accounted for not necessarily in their ability to resist persecution, but in the intermittent character of such persecutions. At first the Sri Lankan government opposed some of the Sarvodaya movement's activities, but now Sarvodaya has won imitation. During the 1971 insurrection, the Christian Workers Fellowship office was closed by the police, and in the 1982 election, government officers came to the office for surveillance. In 1977 the Thai coordinator of the Asian Cultural Forum on Development was advised to stay abroad for a year due to government arrest of students who had some associations with him and other uncertainties. In 1982 a newspaper column he wrote caused the government to threaten the paper. In 1984 he was arrested and detained. However, these crackdowns were intermittent; there has not been continuous persecution by the police or the military.

Goals of Movements for Justice

The movements we consider criticize the present social order primarily in regard to economic injustice; Their goal is economic justice. They have social, cultural, and religious goals as well. In all cases, economic justice is taken as an integral part of the development of persons in community. "Justice" is defined in each movement in terms of its own culture and historical situation. However, it generally includes adequate life sustenance, participation in decision making, dignity and esteem of the person, freedom, and sustainability. Denis Goulet has cogently defined economic development in these terms.[5] He rightly suggests that these goals should be seen in dialectical relationship rather than as a static ordering of ranked values. Further, he points out that, allowing for differences of meaning from culture to culture, "general agreement exists that 'excessive poverty' stunts human lives. . . . Divergent philosophies of life nonetheless concur in certain broad social goals: all regard life as worth protecting, esteem as valuable, and freedom from needless constraints as desirable."[6]

James C. Scott articulates what justice means in practical terms to peasants, tenant farmers, fishermen, and other workers. The peasants' idea of justice is provided by "the norm of reciprocity" and the consequent elite obligation "to guarantee--or at least not infringe upon--the subsistence claims and arrangements of the peasantry."[7] Reciprocity and subsistence are central to the moral or normative understanding of the peasants and their expectations of landowners. Their expectation is that the elite will so reciprocate with them that the village will be able to sustain itself. This is viewed as a social right, and violation of reciprocity and subsistence by the landowner or other elite is looked upon as dissolving the responsibility of the peasant for continued production. When such a violation occurs, indignation and defiance are morally justified.

Such indignation or defiance is, of course, linked to the cultural underpinnings of society. An Asian Cultural Forum on Development publication on peasant theology puts this indignation in its relation to utopian expectations. It points out that there are indeed many degrees of awareness or awakening to one's situation. Then, quoting a Philippine peasant, Mang Paeng (one of the authors) goes on to say that the peasants' awareness or sense of injustice depends "on how involved they are with other peasants and their allies in trying to change the oppressed peasant conditions. . . . It is a heaven that starts on earth."[8] Barrington Moore would add to the moral norms of reciprocity and subsistence the consciousness of "exploitation," which he thinks is objectively sensed as part of the human relationship when the situation "gives to one or more participants systematically and continually much greater advantages and benefits than others."[9]

The role of religion in peasant movements has recently been succinctly discussed by Charles Keyes. He takes James Scott's "norm of reciprocity" and Barrington Moore's "consciousness of exploitation" a step further. While peasants do calculate rationally (according to the norm of reciprocity) in order to maximize the well-being of themselves and their families, they do so on the basis of how value and meaning are articulated in their cultures. "This world is a moral universe in which individual desires, to employ Buddhist language, are to be brought under control by moral reflection on whether one's actions cause suffering to others". He finds that Buddhist villagers in northeastern Thailand "have a distinctive economic ethic, and thus a distinctive moral economy, not because they are peasants, but because they are Buddhists who are peasants".[10]

This study is concerned with movements whose inception came out of religious motivation, teaching, or leadership and whose participants are critical of the present socioeconomic order and work in an organized, sustained effort for a society that will provide life sustenance, dignity, and participation. That may not seem utopian to the affluent world; for much of Asia, justice _is_ utopian.

An explanatory hypothesis for many prophetic movements often has been that large numbers of people were deprived of resources to which they previously had access. The movements we examine have their beginnings largely in response to rural poverty. Another type of explanatory hypothesis is that which views prophetic movements as the products of influences of westernization or Christianity. The syncretic nature of prophetic movements has often been noted. Another way of analysis has been to focus on the leadership of such movements as demonstrating the interaction between the "great" and "little" traditions, of the classical and folk traditions. Indeed, in the case of movements we examine the leadership comes from educated teachers, laymen and clergy who devote themselves to justice issues. Karl Mannheim has provided still another view of religious movements in his distinction between the utopian and the ideological function of religion. THis view has provided the initial conceptualization for this study.

All these hypotheses or ways of examining prophetic utopian movements are worth keeping in mind as we examine the four movements.

II

SOCIAL-CULTURAL SETTING OF CONTEMPORARY RELIGION IN THAILAND AND SRI LANKA

Buddhism in Sri Lanka and Thailand

By the first century A.D. Buddhism in Sri Lanka was already developed, with both scripture and schism. Tradition has it that King Asoka's son Mahinda had come from India with Buddhist teaching in the third century B.C. But in Thailand, although there had been earlier Buddhist contact, Buddhism was not firmly established until the eleventh century A.D.

Thai and Sri Lankan Buddhism share the Pali texts (accepting a recension of 80 B.C. produced in Sri Lanka), the Vinaya monastic discipline, emphasis on Vipasanna meditation, the teachings of no fixed or substantial self (_anatta_), of impermanence (_anicca_), and of the resolution of suffering (_dukkha_) leading to Nirvana. The moral order is related to the cosmic order and the political order in Buddhist thought, myth, and ritual--an important dimension of Buddhism sometimes overlooked in western interpretations.

In both historical and present interpretations, the monkhood has ritual, educational, and spiritual obligations to laypersons.

> The recommended ideal is for monks to be _gramavasi_ (residing in towns and villages and engaging themselves in educational and religious activities) rather than _vanavasi_ (residing in the forest and engaged in meditation with no obligations to the laity).[1]

In Buddhism there is the model of a Sangha adhering strictly to the _Patimokkha_ and _Vinaya_ [ethics for monks] rules. In pristine Buddhism, recruits to the monkhood came from all strata of society and joined together as equals in a community dedicated to simplicity, discipline, and the spiritual quest. The _Patimokkha_ also deals with the interaction between the laity and the monks, indicating an ethic of reciprocity. The monks provide religious instruction and an example of detachment and tranquility; the laymen help provide through alms for the support of the monastery and gain merit. Since the time of Asoka, there is also the tradition of the king purifying the Sangha. In Thailand, Sri Lanka, and Burma, the traditional relationship between the Buddhist temple and the village was disrupted by colonialism, westernization, and, more recently, urbanization. The leadership of the temple abbot and the monks has declined with the development of a commercial and utilitarian society. All religions in times of crisis or transition may need to go back to their early sources of inspiration or to a supposedly more golden era for a sense of direction and cohesion. Thus at times a first step forward to meet this disorganizing incursion may be a step back to a more pristine ethic and to a Sangha that in order to regain its identity may temporarily withdraw from society or assert itself in ways that are more rigid, or even nationalistic. This may be a defense mechanism against western commercialism and cultural influences as well as a reinvigoration of the Sangha's own roots.

The contemporary social-cultural settings of Buddhism in Thailand and Sri Lanka differ. Sri Lanka suffered over four hundred years of colonialism under the Portuguese, the Dutch, and the British. But Thailand, except for Japanese occupation during the second World War, has been free of overt foreign domination.

Religious consequences of colonialism

Colonialism in Sri Lanka was accompanied with foreign missions and periods of special privileges to Christian schools. Christians are now about 8 percent of the population, with a greater proportion in urban areas. (The Christian Workers Fellowship took root in Colombo.) Proximity to India and British importation of Indian laborers has resulted in a population which is 18 percent Hindu. The Indian Tamil tea plantation workers are in a doubly vulnerable position, being noncitizens and poor. Muslims comprise 7 percent of the total. Thus, Sinhala Buddhists, with 67 percent of the population, are the dominant group, but in a pluralistic setting. It is sometimes said in Sri Lanka that the Buddhists are a majority who think like a minority.

The Portuguese brought Catholic missions to Sri Lanka; the Dutch persecuted Catholics and forbade the Mass. In British times there was religious freedom, but the British patronized the Anglican church. As Father Balasuryia tells us,

> Many of the local families that benefited from the economic development under the British were Christians. Proportionately there were more Christians among the planters, public servants, merchants, executives, and professionals. The centers of affluence were the urban areas, especially in the western coastal belt. Here Christians were in larger numbers.[2]

The imposition of European colonialism and the privileged position given to Christians aroused Buddhist demands for cultural, legal, and religious recognition. The efforts of Colonel H. S. Olcott (an American Buddhist) and Sri Lankan Anagarika Dharmapala aroused a kind of religionationalism and awakened the Buddhist community in the late 1800s.

As S. J. Tambiah suggests, "It is well known that the missionary presence has acted as an irritant and has produced a counter-response in the world religions of Southeast Asian countries."[3] Christian proselytism produced at least four responses in Southeast Asian societies: (1) a reform or purifying of some of their "gross" practices, (2) the assertion of a rational and modern religion supposedly validated by ancient scripture, (3) a counterattack to what was irrational and superstitious in Christianity, and (4) the use of propagation techinques, such as printing, of the westerners.[4] Tension has run high between Buddhists and Christians in Sri Lanka at times, largely over the favored position of Christian institutions under colonialism. The secularization of schools continues.

Thailand is much more homogeneous, with 95 percent of its population Buddhist, 4 percent Muslim, and less than 1 percent Christian. Its three southern provinces of Thailand have a larger Muslim population, and political-religious movements for separatism have spawned violence and helped fuel the cause of leftist insurgents in the area. It was during the reign of King Rama III (r. 1824-1851) that Thailand was pressured into treaties of trade with Britain and the United States. The first Protestant missionaries came in 1828, two years after the signing of the first treaty. Although Rama III's successor, Mongkut, had an avid interest in western science and technology and in Christian theology, he assumed that a revitalized Buddhism could stand up to any challenge they presented. Catholic missionaries had come to Thailand in the seventeenth century, but their presence was not to be permanent and expanded until after 1830.[5]

The Buddhist Monkhood in Sri Lanka and Thailand

The Sri Lankan Sangha is unfortunately divided by caste. Some groups do not admit to higher ordination persons who lack favored caste status. Abbots in some instances seem to favor installing relatives as their successors to keep temple property within family control. (Castes were the result of comparatively late infusions into Sri Lanka, probably the result of migration from India between the thirteenth and eighteenth centuries.) However, it was the upward social mobility of lower castes in the first part of the nineteenth century that produced new groups or "chapters" in the Sangha. This "sect" movement resulted in a number of caste-based groups, and in 1844 a noncaste, reform-minded sect, the Ramanna Nikaya, was established.

The reform movement in Thailand, the Thammayut sect, on the other hand, came out of the work of Prince Mongkut and the government. The Thai Sangha has been relatively free of social class discrimination, although the royalty or nobility patronized favored monasteries. Traditionally, the Thai Sangha has recruited heavily in rural areas and provided a means of education and social mobility for young men. Only a third of Thai monks are "permanent" monks; many are ordained for a short time. Sri Lankan monks traditionally follow a lifetime vocation, although secular education recently appears to increase the incidence of disrobing.

The monkhood in Sri Lanka has often looked to the government for support, but it is free of government control. As a matter of fact, the Sangha, it is often said, lacks coordination and organization. In Thailand, on the other hand, the monkhood is organized into a hierarchical structure under a government department of religious affairs. The monarchy continues as a strong national symbol and a force for national unity. (In Sri Lanka the British dislodged the Kandyan Kings in 1815, and there is no equivalent symbol or force such as the Thai monarchy.)

Poverty and Urbanization in Sri Lanka and Thailand

The village has been the natural habitat of Buddhism in both countries. The temple, the tank (irrigation reservoir), and the paddy field are three symbols of Sri Lankan culture that are prominent even today. Both countries are still predominantly rural. Sri Lanka is 19 percent urban; Thailand is 21 percent. Rampant growth in Bangkok in the last twenty years presents a far greater problem of inmigration than it does any other city in the country. Urban wats are having a difficult time finding a constructive role to play. Population growth, together with rural poverty, is likely to increase urbanization. The dominance of Bangkok is often emphasized. Today about one out of every ten Thais lives in Bangkok, whose population is 5,494,000. Almost 90 percent of the automobiles in the country are registered there. The metropolitan area is more than forty times larger than Chiang Mai, Thailand's second city. There are at present 300 areas classified as slum or squatter areas providing homes for 700,000 to 800,000 persons. Public services such as water, fire protection, sanitation, and education are substandard, to say the least. It is reported that as many as 200,000 children between eleven and fourteen are employed in Bangkok's factories.

The concentration of political and economic power in Bangkok has led to an emphasis on urban and industrial development, largely at the expense of the farmer. For a time following World War II the government controlled rice export; since returning it to private hands in 1955, the government has manipulated the price of rice through an export tax.

Colombo, the primate city of Sri Lanka, has increased in population from 154,000 in 1901 to about 600,000 at present. The rate of urbanization in Sri Lanka has not been as rapid as in other developing countries--certainly not as dramatic as in Bangkok. However, housing and public services are major problems. About 50 percent of Colombo's population live in slums or shanties. Only 60 percent of the households benefit from piped-in home water, and only 22 percent have pipe-borne sewerage. In some sections of the city as many as 500 persons have to bathe from one tap. It is estimated that approximately 50,000 children of the poorer income groups in Colombo are permanently stunted from malnutrition and disease.

While no one really knows the incidence of child labor in Colombo, it is estimated that 26 percent of the children do not go to school at all; another 47 percent complete only up to grade five.

Rural Poverty in Thailand and Sri Lanka

Landless or near-landless rural workers in both Thailand and Sri Lanka are not as numerous as in some other Asian countries. Bangladesh, Indonesia, Pakistan, and the Philippines all have between 89 percent and 81 percent dispossessed. Landless laborers compose 50 percent of the Thai rural population and 73 percent of the rural population in Sri Lanka.[6] The land shortage is particularly acute in Sri Lanka's hill country, where the tea plantations were established. In Thailand one of the main reasons for landlessness among farmers is that middle-class and wealthy urbanites have bought up land, particularly in the central region.[7] In both countries indebtedness among farmers is widespread and chronic. Although the percentage of the population considered to be in "absolute poverty" in both countries has decreased recently, conservative estimates are that at least 20 percent of Sri Lankans and 25 percent of Thais are in that category.

> Poverty may be broadly defined as a condition wherein the flow of consumable resources available to a household falls short of a minimum that is deemed necessary for its members to meet their essential needs so as to be able to maintain their productive capacity and enjoy a minimum of well-being. A sense of well-being is in its essence something that is subjective although it rests on physical and material considerations. Any measurement of poverty, however, has to fall back on using some objective indicators and the subjective experience of poverty are not the same thing. . . . But we can with a little more certainty arrive at a level of Absolute poverty in terms of firm indicators when we take absolute poverty as the inability to enjoy a diet that provides a minimum recommended nutrition in terms of bare calories and proteins.[8]

However, the most pressing economic and social problems in both countries arise from major regional imbalances in the distribution of income. In the poorest regions such as the dry northeast area of Thailand, 38 percent are in "absolute poverty," and in the rural plantation areas between Kandy and Ratnapura in Sri Lanka, 29 percent of the population are so considered.[9] To some extent an ethnic and linguistic issue may add to the complexity of the problem of poverty. Northeast Thailand is influenced by Lao culture, and it is geographically somewhat removed from the dominance of Bangkok. The Tamils in Sri Lanka, particularly those on the tea plantations, are deprived of adequate housing, health facilities, and education. The rural sections adjacent to the plantations seem to be among the poorest in income and nutrition.[10]

Problems of Economic Justice in Sri Lanka and Thailand

The dilemma between economic efficiency and equity, between aggregate growth and social welfare, is a persistent economic and moral problem for government planners and policy makers in third world countries. For many years Sri Lanka leaned toward enhancing the general welfare through public expenditures for education and health care and providing rice subsidies. The present government, which came to power in 1977, has encouraged private enterprise, foreign investment, free trade zones, and tourism. (Singapore is spoken of favorably as a model.) Consumer goods for the middle class are more plentiful. Vast irrigation projects are under way in the Mahaweli River area to increase agricultural productivity. Because of the long-standing emphasis on education and health, the Physical Quality of Life Index (PQLI) of Sri Lanka has been estimated at 80 by the Overseas Development Council in 1982. (This measurement combines life expectancy, infant mortality, and literacy rates.) This despite the fact that the per capita annual income is equivalent to only $270 in U.S. currency. This gives Sri Lanka the highest PQLI among the low-income countries. Nevertheless, there is the persistent issue of the 25 percent who still live in absolute poverty and the 50 percent or so who suffer from malnutrition.

In Thailand the per capita income is considerably higher, equivalent to U.S. $670, but the PQLI, at 75, is a little lower than Sri Lanka's. This reflects the attention given in Sri Lanka to health care. Infant mortality is considerably higher in Thailand. The expenditure in Thailand per capita for health is among the lowest in the so-called "middle-income" countries.[11] The growth rate as an annual percentage of GNP between 1970 and 1980 has been very similar, 6.97 in Sri Lanka and 7.0 in Thailand. Development theorists have held that economic development may initially lead to enlarged inequality. Even though all may gain, the rich, particularly in urban areas, may benefit by getting a much higher proportion of the total pie. This disproportion can be bearable only if the overall growth rate is rapid. Gunnar Myrdal has suggested that Western economists have assumed "a conflict between economic growth and egalitarian reforms. They take it for granted that a price has to be paid for reforms and that often this price is prohibitive for poor countries."[12] He attributes this bias to "the moral philosophies of a natural law and utilitarianism out of which economic theory once branched off."[13] The regional distribution of income, already noted demonstrates the great inequality and injustice that exists in both Thailand and Sri Lanka. Although the percentage of the population judged to be in absolute poverty has decreased, since malnutrition estimates are about 50 percent of the populace, deeper problems are evident.[14]

Politics in Sri Lanka and Thailand

Universal suffrage was achieved in Sri Lanka in 1934. Since 1948, when independence was gained from the British, the government has changed six times, all by way of elections. In 1971 a violent insurrection involving some students and led by a Peking-oriented political group was quickly suppressed. It has been charged that the most recent election in 1982 was so manipulated that its democratic nature is questionable. The chief opposition candidate was prevented from running, and government harassment of opposition forces was common. The Christian Workers Fellowship offices (the CWF will be examined later in this study) in Colombo were visited twice by government officers, and their organizer in Hatton was beaten.

In 1932 the absolute monarchy in Thailand was transformed into what has been called "Thai-style democracy." In practice, final power, which once resided in the monarchy, has fallen into the hands of groups of government bureaucrats and the military. Farmer unions, industrial unions, and student groups have been blocked from effective countervailing action. Private enterprise has joined forces with the government, using its economic position to maintain its ascendancy. In 1973 a democratically inspired student uprising led to a brief period of reform. The political inexperience of the students was one cause of the resurgence of political and military forces on the right. A protest by students at Thammasat University in 1976 was put down with bloodshed by the army. The military continues to play a leading role in the political arena.

Recent Social Upheaval in Sri Lanka and Thailand

Both countries during the last decade have experienced social upheaval and a spectrum of socioreligious movements, including conservative nationalistic, moderate reforming, and utopian and radically critical groups. Thailand has felt the threat of Communist neighbors with wars going on in Vietnam, Laos, and Kampuchea. Communists are said to be active among the Muslim minority in the south. The Thai government has followed American foreign policy and maintained allegiance to the West in the world power struggle. American military aid has provided the army with a strong grip on society and enabled it to suppress militant opposition. But Sri Lanka has had little or no threat from any foreign military force. This may partly explain the greater openness in discussing and advocating Marxism among some intellectuals and monks. European socialism in a variety of forms has influenced Sri Lanka; indeed, democratic socialism is the norm for the majority political parties. Gandhi has also influenced religious and political movements.

In both countries some monks have exhibited zealous conservative and militant nationalism. In Thailand, Kittiwutho Bhikku has defended the killing of communists as a defense of the nation and an act of Buddhist merit.[15] During a 1958 dispute over the language to be used for official government matters in Sri Lanka, Buddhist monks were "among the most vociferous advocates of Sinala only."[16] This dispute over language eventually led to the outbreaks of violence and tension that continue even now between the Tamil minority and the Sinhala Buddhists.

During the sixties and seventies there was a maturing critical consciousness of dependency and exploitation among peoples of impoverished nations, races, classes, and social groups. Elements within the intelligentsia of dominant nations and groups also recognized the injustice and untenability of the policies of their own nations and made some efforts to cooperate with oppressed people. In international religious organizations there was some response. Vatican II brought a new attitude toward non-Christian religions and since John XXIII a religious philosophy of fundamental social change has evolved. The World Council of Churches has enunciated a goal for a "just, participatory, and sustainable" social order and has established a very active Churches Commission on Participatory Development. The World Fellowship of Buddhists, generally not in the vanguard of social criticism, was able to hold a world conference in Colombo on the theme "Survival and Development." Delegations from the Peoples Republic of China and the USSR participated.

At the grass-roots level, Joel S. Migdal has commented:

> As the world outside shrinks, the peasants' political world expands. New problems arise that cannot be solved inside the village; the locus for decision making shifts to the district, province, and state. Because of this peasants in many places have begun to participate in rallies, demonstrations and political movements.[17]

With this summary of similarities and differences in the religious, economic, and social conditions in Thailand and Sri Lanka, we are ready to turn to the contemporary scene and look at four movements that exemplify some of the socioreligious ferment now taking place in those countries.

III

THE SARVODAYA SHRAMADANA MOVEMENT

Sarvodaya Shramadana is the most successful Buddhist movement for development and justice in Asia. Its growth over a period of twenty-eight years and its work and influence in more than two thousand villages in Sri Lanka are notable achievements. Its personable yet hardheaded founder and president, Ahangamage Tudor Ariyaratne, has received the Ramon Magsaysay award, among other tributes. Wapola Rahula, an eminent Buddhist scholar, is proposing him for the Nobel Peace Prize. There are few, if any, religious movements of national dimension that have as broad an impact in Asia. Although its influence and reputation have grown, it has suffered over the past decade from the growth of its own bureacracy, its difficulty in decentralizing its program and keeping accountability, and its increasing cooperation with the government.

The Sarvodaya vision is a profound and challenging one. _Sarvodaya Shramadana_ can be translated as "the awakening of all through the sharing of labor." It begins with striving to awaken individuals to the fullest realization of their own personalities (_purna paurushodaya_), moves on to awakening groups and villages (_gramadaya_), then to stimulating concrete action at the national level (_deshodaya_), and finally to generating worldwide awakening and development (_vishvodaya_).

It was apparent in Sri Lanka in the spring of 1982 that the international influence of the movement was significant. Visitors from Africa, Malaysia, Canada, France, and the United States came to participate, learn, and listen. Since 1969 there has been a "village-to-village linkup" program beginning with Belgium and now extending to villages in the Netherlands, New Zealand, and Canada. Sarvodaya has an international network of exchange personnel for training, information, and research. Ariyaratne himself has had to restrict accepting invitations from around the world.

The Philosophy of Sarvodaya

The headquarters of Sarvodaya Shramadana just north of Colombo abounds in plaques and posters enunciating its program and principles. One such sign displayed prominently, proclaims its assessment of "the present social order":

> Worships wealth, power, and position and uses untruth, violence, and selfishness. Organizations based on possession and vicious competition become strong. Capitalistic economy, bureaucratic control, power and party politics become major social forces.
>
> Dependence on import-export economy based on colonially inherited patterns of production of cash crops foreign debts increase.

Ariyaratne in his younger days had shown interest in radical political movements. He was once a candidate of the Communist party. However, his idealism and energy were more profoundly shaped by Vinoba Bhave and Gandhian social thought. As a teacher, he once organized his students in a nonviolent protest "satyagraha"-style to demonstrate against the interference of a government official in the school. A large portrait of Gandhi dominates his headquarters office. Bhave's Bhoodan-Gramdan movement and Gandhi's philosophy of "the welfare of all" were the initial inspirations to Sarvodaya. Building on them, Ariyaratne writes that:

> The Sarvodaya philosophy is a synthetic ideology and universal concept. All forms of creative altruism and evolutionary humanism, be it from marxian aim of material integration, Rousseau's option of social integration or Asoka's endeavor of moral integration . . . are inherent in Sarvodaya's philosophy practiced by us.[1]

This synthesis seems to be increasingly expressed in a Buddhistic way. The four noble truths and the eightfold path are repeated in Sarvodayan writings. Particularly prominent is the use of the Brahma-Viharas (the four sublime Abodes): (1) Metta (loving-kindness); (2) Karuna (compassion); (3) Muditha (altruistic joy); (4) Upekkha (equanimity).

A recent and fuller interpretation of the Brahma-Vihara by Ariyaratne is as follows:

(i) Respect for all life (Metta).
(ii) Compassionate action (Karuna) to remove all constraints that prevent the awakening of human personalities to the fullest.
(iii) Learning to experience the dispassionate joy (Muditha) that one gets when involved in such compassionate action.
(iv) Development of psychologically balanced personalities or persons with equanimity (Upekkha).[2]

In one of his early speeches Ariyaratne makes the distinction between "the welfare of All" as a principle of Buddhist thought and the utilitarian view of "the Greatest Good of the Greatest Number." The "Welfare of All"--the Buddhist teaching "May All Beings be well and Happy"--stresses the good of the whole society and of each person rather than the development of some at possible cost to others. To be "awakened" is to realize that one has a role in the harmonious development of all. Enlightenment means continuous new self-knowledge and growing service to fellow human beings.[3] Viewing the concrete historical actions of Vinoba Bhave and Mahatma Gandhi, Ariyaratne advocates nonviolent direct action in a voluntary "revolution from below" as his guide to Sarvodaya at work. He emphasizes again and again the necessity of revolutionary change beginning in the individual and moving in expanding circles to the family, the village, the nation, and the world. He maintains that change can be accomplished through a network of self-supporting villages rather than through party politics. The fragmentation and occasional stridency of Sri Lankan political parties is certainly part of the reason for Ariyaratne's deemphasizing the role of political parties.

The concept of awakening applies to every individual, but the primary effort in development "should be to fulfill without delay the social, economic and spiritual aspirations of that segment of society which stands lowest in it."[4] This concept is called antyodaya or "the awakening of the lowliest, lowest and the lost in the society."[5] Indeed, the practice of Sarvodaya has been to focus its work on some of the poorest and most underprivileged communities in the country. Ariyaratne comments that the word antyodaya is the Sanskritized word that Mahatma Gandhi used in India to translate Ruskin's "unto this last."[6] He interprets the Buddhist term tanha (attachment or thirst) as acquistiveness in human beings. Gautama Buddha rejected acquisitiveness but encouraged dana or sharing. Ariyaratne explains further:

> If the motivating force in the mind is Metta or respect for all lives then a human being who accepts this principle has to necessarily translate this thought into concrete action called 'Karuna.' We are helping a landless cultivator to liberate himself from the bondage imposed on him by unscrupulous landowners not because we hate the landowner but because we love or respect the life of the poor landless cultivator. . . .
>
> We are not prepared to concede revolutionary monopoly only to those who base all their social actions on organized hatred. We have based our revolutionary approach on Loving Kindness and the organization of compassionate action. It is impossible to build up just and righteous societies without a high level of spirituality even under most trying and exploitative situations.[7]

The Beginning of the Movement

In 1958 A.T. Ariyaratne was one of a number of teachers and students at a Buddhist high school in Colombo that organized a work camp in Kanatholuwa, one of the poorest villages of Sri Lanka, to provide a real-life experience for students and to work with people of depressed areas in self-help community service projects. A close friend of Ariyaratne's, D.A. Abeyesekera, a rural development officer, returned from a stay in Europe with reports of work camps organized by the Quakers. The Quaker precedent inspired and guided the first Shramadana work camps.[8] The government had earlier attempted to send teachers into some poor Sri Lankan villages, but this effort did not succeed, Ariyaratne says, because the teachers did not understand that they had to be taught first before they could teach.[9] Within the first ten years of Sarvodaya Shramadana, thousands of volunteers, from both urban and rural areas, were attracted to work in this form of community development.

The Development of the Movement

There are roughly three periods in Sarvodaya's history. The first phase, from its inception to about 1962, was a period employing the Shramadana (sharing of labor) volunteer work camps as their main method and program. The majority of those working with the villagers were middle-class and relatively well educated, many from towns or urban areas. In their projects some education went along with digging wells for pure drinking water, repairing irrigation tanks, constructing latrines and waste disposal facilities, footpaths and roads, and, in some cases, attempting rural electrification.

The second phase began in the early sixties, when a more systematic effort was introduced to widen the impact on villages. Villages began to affiliate with Sarvodaya for longer terms and to make integrated plans for development. Systematic efforts were made to renew relationships among Buddhist temples, monks, and villagers. Specialized volunteers and village leaders were recruited and trained. The program developed a more complex organizational structure.

The Sarvodaya process developed and systematized in the sixties consisted of four stages: (1) understanding the problem (including a survey of village resources and needs); (2)

building village organizations (with emphasis on age groups, farmers' groups and health care); (3) establishing village services (including schools, credit unions, temples, and so on); and (4) initiating development activities. The goal of this process was to meet ten basic needs:

1. A clean and beautiful environment
2. A safe and adequate supply of water
3. Basic requirements of clothing
4. A regular and balanced diet
5. A simple abode
6. Basic health care services
7. Transport and communication facilities
8. Fuel
9. Continuing education for all
10. Cultural and spiritual development

These ten basic needs have been subdivided into 165 subneeds.[10]

This amplification of basic needs demonstrates the comprehensive nature of Sarvodaya philosophy as well as its grass-roots context. For example, "a clean and beautiful environment" is subdivided into sixty different particulars having to do with the house, the home garden, the latrine, the well, public roads, and so on. Sections on the home apply to the kitchen, the sleeping room, the visitors' room, the storeroom, and the like. Statement 35 suggests that a raised shelf "for placing the water pot" be provided. The pot's "mouth should be covered with an earthen vessel. (When covered with a coconut shell there is the risk of crows upsetting it and inserting their beaks into the water pot, thus contaminating the water in the pot.)"[11]

The third period began in 1968. The period from then through the seventies witnessed rapid expansion, increased foreign support, and the use of a full-time staff. Some Shramadana camps specialized in education, vocational training, and distress relief in addition to their regular programs. In the early seventies Sarvodaya began an ambitious preschool and mothers' group program in low-income villages. A Bhikkhu (monk) training center with good facilities was established at Pathakada with support from a German foundation in 1975. In the six years of its operation, 350 monks participated in a four- or six-month course. Short-term courses were also provided. The purpose of the program was to train monks in all aspects of the total Sarvodaya program so that they could provide leadership and articulate the movement's methods and goals in their home villages. The move to develop a hundred villages in 1968 broadened to include a thousand in 1975.

During this third period of Sarvodaya's development, in 1971, a dissident group in Sri Lanka attempted a violent insurrection. Many of the insurrectionists were educated youth from rural areas. The insurrection, although unsuccessful, awakened the nation to the frustrations of some of the young. Some youths disillusioned with the violence evidently found meaning in some of the Sarvodaya programs.

Shramadana Work Camps

Shramadana work camps now are likely to be under way at many places on the island at almost any time. Since 1978 the number of work camps has grown from about seven hundred to over a thousand a year. Sundays seem to be the most popular days because people are not working at regular jobs. With enough people, a couple of miles of dirt roads can be roughed out in a Sunday or two--not easy work in areas of tropical growth. Elephants may help with heavier work like moving logs, but no mechanical earthmoving equipment is used. Roads and footpaths are important in getting children to school, food to local markets, and the sick to clinics. A Sarvodaya motto expresses the work camp philosophy: "We build the road and the road builds us."

Since the camp is part of an educational effort to build community solidarity, all are involved--young and old, men and women. Ariyaratne tells of soliciting food for the Shramadana workers before one of the first camps. A well-off landowner volunteered to supply all that was necessary, but Ariyaratne asked for other contributions in order to share and spread the responsibility. "Dana" or giving is not the privilege or responsibility of a few of the "better off" in society. Often the village temple is used as an organizing center, and donations of food are supplied as part of "dana" for the shramadana workers. People come to assist from other villages, occasionally crossing caste lines. Students may come from one of the university campuses.

From the early sixties planning for Shramadana camps has been guided by a survey of the villages' needs, their resources, and the readiness of village people to participate. (Sarvodaya has not been able to respond to all the requests from the village for the movement's assistance.) A typical camp takes much preparation--meeting with the village elders, monks, teachers, doctors, and others to insure sound participation and support. Such preparation may reveal conflicts that must be faced. For example, decisions on developing irrigation ditches may require dealing with larger landowners and attempting to see that the existing power structure in a village is not simply reinforced. Obviously, such decisions are not easily made. The tendency to defer to the landed elite or others in the power structure is not changed simply by the decision to hold a work camp. "Trickle down" may well exist as a reflex of development in the village power structure.

Religious rituals in Sarvodaya activities are more in evidence at the Shramadana work camps than elsewhere in the Sarvodaya program. A Shramadana camp is inaugurated the evening before the actual start of work with the lighting of the traditional coconut oil lamp, the chanting of "Pirith" Buddhist Sutras, the singing of Sarvodaya songs, and the raising of the national and Sarvodaya flags. Following this there is a "family gathering," in some ways the heart of the Shramadana experience. All the villagers sit on straw mats in a circle to discuss the village's needs and problems and explore ways to resolve them. A Sarvodaya leader may initiate the discussion, but volunteers from the outside come to listen and learn, not to teach. Leaders try to involve different age groups in the discussion and to encourage participation beyond the ordinary status barriers. During the camp, family gatherings occupy about four hours of the day--two hours after lunch and two following dinner. Singing, dancing, and readings from traditional religious teachers are intermixed with more serious discussion on community, national, and even international problems. Decisions on work and work assignments are usually made at the family gatherings after the evening meal. A short period of meditation ends the evening.

Shramadana camps may last from a day to a month. Over 13,000 such camps were conducted in the period from 1971 to 1981. Sarvodaya headquarters reports that more than 170,000 participated in camps in 1981. Participants number from twenty-five to two or three hundred, depending on the size of the village and the type of project undertaken: making roads or paths can absorb more labor than digging wells.

Bhikkhu Training Institute

A community leadership training institute of Buddhist monks was established in 1972 and a regular ongoing training program in 1975. The latter coincided with the establishment of a center at Pathakada in the south-central section of the island near the city of Ratnapura. The site is somewhat isolated. It has six simple but functional buildings constructed with support from the Friedrich Nauman Stiftung Foundation of Germany. Dormitories accommodate sixty trainee monks. A classroom and a dining hall are part of the "campus". The Sri Lankan Buddhist tradition, some twenty centuries old, is a proud and generally respected one, and the Sangha continues to play an important role in the culture. Sarvodaya both gains from its association with the Sangha and contributes to it by providing the monks with a renewed community function.

Ideally, Bhikkhus return to their home villages after the training program and engage in development work as well as traditional religious activities. The institute itself conducts Shramadana camps and initiates other Sarvodaya projects. In 1976-77, for example, twenty-eight Shramadana camps were held under the Bhikkhu Training Institute's direction, and twenty preschools and twenty-three community kitchens were established.

The training period, from four to six months long, includes courses in Sarvodaya philosophy, community organization, public health, and practical agriculture. There are also courses in social welfare services, management, English, astrology and working with government contacts in the village. Short-term courses, for a number of weeks or a month, are also offered. From 1974 to 1976, 149 monks were trained in the long-term courses, and some 350 in shorter programs.

Dr. Nandasena Ratnapala, director of the Sarvodaya Research Institute, has reflected on several problems that have emerged in the Bhikkhu Training Program. First, in recruiting monks for the training, too little attention has been paid to leadership qualities or to motivation for village development activities. Indeed, recruiting has now shifted to seeking monks who already have worked for some time in Sarvodaya-related activities in their villages because young monks or novices with no involvement in the movement lack the experience to make the best use of the training program. There have been some who, having taken university entrance examinations, simply enroll in Bhikkhu training as a way to fill their time until they are admitted to the University. There has also been some disparity in background and education among the recruits, who come from all parts of the country. These differences have made for uneven ability to work in the program.

Second, a follow-up program to assist newly trained monks has been lacking. They need supervision and encouragement in beginning their efforts in their villages. Returning to their villages, they may find older Bhikkhus unable to relate to new ideas and ways of working in the village. So a continuing education program has recently been launched to interpret the Sarvodaya approach in a more effective way to older monks who will work with the training program graduates.

Third, teachers at the Bhikkhu Training Center in some instances have lacked either academic qualifications or adequate experience in village development concerns. Obviously, the success of the program depends on people with a combination of practical skills, motivation of the Buddhist faith, and leadership ability to empower people to work in difficult situations in poor villages. This is a demanding task! Dr. Ratnapala has commented that: "the monk's role in the past had not been confined only to the teaching of religion. Sarvodaya decided to identify this neglected role, resuscitate it and redefine it to fit in with the changing times and new technology."[12] Dr. Ratnapala's critical evaluation is a hopeful indication of Sarvodaya's ability to examine its own program realistically and to learn from its own mistakes.

The Bhikkhu Training Program at Pathakada is only one aspect of the involvement of monks in the work of Sarvodaya. Joanna Macy in her field work found that Bhikkhus in many villages had a number of important roles in Sarvodaya: (1) They often are a key in introducing Sarvodaya Shramadana work. (2) They function frequently in an instructional capacity providing information on everything from brick making and herbal medicine to Buddhist philosophy. (3) They serve as community organizers initiating tea-marketing cooperatives, social service activities, literacy classes, and so on. Macy has also found a renewed interest in Buddhist meditation among monks related to the Sarvodaya program.[13] In addition to their activities within the village, Bhikkhus frequently serve as go-betweens with government officials. My observation is that they also provide a sensitive voice within the Sarvodaya organization itself. The Buddhist Sangha is a separate organization from the Sarvodaya movement and Bhikkhus have a degree of detachment and independence from outside control. They constitute a communication network within Sarvodaya independent of the sometimes bureaucratic nature of the organization. At the same time Sarvodaya offers the means of renewing the integral role of the Sangha in the villages. However, the monks role may be greatest in the early stages of Sarvodaya's development in the village and may lessen once the program becomes fully developed and lay leadership grows.

I have emphasized the Shramadana Work Camps and the Bhikkhu Training Center. Certainly the Shramadana camps continue to be the growing edge of the movement. In 1980 and 1981 over three thousand work camps were held throughout the country. The emphasis now seems to be on shorter camps with smaller groups. In 1980 and 1981 about half the projects were for two to three days with more than fifty participants. Somewhat fewer than half the camps were organized especially for students in order to broaden their understanding of village needs, to foster their appreciation of the music, dance and drama of the village culture, and to expose them to religious diversity.[14]

In addition to the Shramadana camps and the Bhikkhu Insitutes there are other dimensions to the work of Sarvodaya.

Sarvodaya Gramadaya Centers--about 150 in all--coordinate village work within a radius of five to ten miles each. Their most important function is leadership training and education. They also initiate and coordinate health activities in over 1,500 preschools. More than 22,000 children were provided immunization in 1981. Community kitchens, organized along with the preschools, have served supplemental food, milk, and juice to thousands of young children. As part of the preschool program, youth and mothers are trained in child care, nutrition, hygiene and health care. Of the children examined in preschools, 22 percent to 58 percent suffer from anemia. (The variation in percentages comes from spot checks of 4,000 to 12,000 children in different quarters of the year.)

The Gramadaya Centers also encourage the "family gathering" of all members of the community as a regular instrument of village awakening. Mothers' groups, youth groups, and farmers' groups are fostered as part of community development.

Sarvodaya also operates twenty-two farms as part of its program. The earliest was established in 1970. The farms vary in size from one-and-a-half acres to fifty acres. During periods of drought some of them cannot operate. Three of the farm projects encourage homestead vegetable gardening; the others serve as change agents in fusing appropriate agricultural technology with traditional farming methods. They also employ the village youth and give them leadership training. Some farms have a connection with the village Buddhist temple, whose abbot provides leadership. Ten of the farms are on land owned by the government; the others are on private land. Funds for developing the farms come from the central Sarvodaya organization.

There are other Sarvodaya programs, but these exemplify the movement's thrust, style, and achievements.

Criticisms of Sarvodaya

Sarvodaya has its critics. Denis Goulet, scholar of development ethics, in Survival With Integrity: Sarvodaya at the Crossroads, (Colombo, Marga Institute, 1981) poses important questions. First, he asks how a movement can maintain its adherence to self-reliance while it accepts substantial assistance from foreign foundations. Second, he wonders if Sarvodaya can develop "macrocriticism" of the Sri Lankan social order and challenge the existing order to change. He doubts that the interpretation of nonviolence as forgoing confrontation and conflict in the political arena is adequate. Goulet suggests that in using the term "total revolution," Sarvodaya shows its rejection of elite and Western models of development; yet it avoids "frontal assaults" or confrontation with its opponents.[15]

The charge that Sarvodaya does not provide a "macro-criticism" or "structural analysis" of the social order suggests that it ignores the growing urban and industrial sector and does not openly oppose the present government's policies of encouraging a free-trade zone, an increasingly capitalist economic order, and a consumer society.

Ariyaratne speaks of the movement being self-reliant but not self-sufficient. (The movement aims for financial independence by the end of 1985.) However, if the volunteer hours of labor in Shramadana camps were quantified, estimates of self-reliance would vastly increase. Further, the terms of donations from foreign groups are negotiated to fit Sarvodaya's needs and ways of work. Ariyaratne also suggests that economic inequity existed for over four hundred years under colonialism and that righting this imbalance is not at all inequitable so long as the direction is clearly toward self-reliance.

District leaders meeting in April of 1982 discussed the possibility of Sarvodaya assuming a more direct political role. A number of Bhikkhus at the training center said that the chief opposition to Sarvodaya in some villages came from the J.V.P. party (Jathika Vimukthi Peramuna or the Sinhalese National Liberation Front), a Trotskyite group. These Bhikkhus were looking for some articulate response. However, the leaders of Sarvodaya have resisted using political parties as a vehicle for the "total revolution." Ariyaratne envisions the movement eventually spreading in influence from the grass roots until the people control important decisions. In 1977 Ariyaratne, in an address to the International Council on Social Welfare, explains:

> We should not be dazzled by the monstrous structures that we see around us, be they bureaucratic, militaristic, or otherwise in nature. . . . What is needed are grass-roots actions in thousands of places in the world, showing by example a new pattern of total education and new ways of development participation where man and his human values are right at the heart of our work. . . . Lack of grass-roots initiative and leadership is one of the main sources of the present unbalanced nature of our society.[16]

It is not clear how this process of grass-roots change will affect problems of international trade, the free trade zone, urbanization, and other issues that are now dealt with by the political machinery.

The remarkable late Anglican Bishop Lakshman Wickremesinghe, a friendly critic of Sarvodaya, asked whether any elite families in Sarvodaya villages have responded by changing the unfair system of shares between laborers and landowners or whether the well-to-do have changed less usurious interest on loans to the poor.

He suspected that the elite often welcome increased productivity and may even look benevolently on Sarvodaya, since it has not disrupted the caste-ridden feudal framework. He went on to ask whether "development" in the Buddhist scriptures and in the indigenous cultural tradition actually means benevolent paternalism. He commented that Ariyaratne rarely refers to oppression or to exploitation or to nonviolence as a revolutionary force for transferring wealth and power from the elite to the marginalized or the poor in the society.[17]

On the other hand, Joanna Macy thinks that Sarvodaya is an Asian-Buddhist form of the "social gospel," a parallel to "liberation theology" in the West.[18] "As has been occured in regard to the teachings of Jesus, the Buddha's teachings on social equality and political participation are being brought to the fore as a challenge--to inspire not just enlightenment of individuals but the transformation of society itself."[19]

Sarvodaya, at first opposed by some government officials, came to be imitated by the government and now cooperates with it. Whether it will be able to maintain creative tension with a government that is now encouraging private enterprise and multinational investment is yet to be seen.

Western-style nationalism in Asian countries has often followed the lead of westernized intellectuals and failed to evoke a response from the subsoil of society--peasants, fishermen, and workers. Sarvodaya penetration of the rural agricultural society of Sri Lanka may be an instance of what Clifford Geertz describes as the "integrative revolution," the reassertion of primordial groups successfully interweaving their form of nationalism into the fabric of contemporary society. Whether or not Sarvodaya can form links with other subsocieties, the Tamils and industrial workers may determine the effectiveness of this "integrative revolution."[20]

The history of Sarvodaya illustrates how a group moves from early idealism, when all work is done by volunteers, to an established organization with government recognition. Mrs. Ariyaratne handled all the office work in the first years--in addition to raising six children. Movements like

Sarvodaya sometimes experience the paradox that Max Weber called "the routinization of charisma." Government sanction of Sarvodaya may push it from utopia to ideology. Sarvodaya has not yet become ideological in Mannheim's sense; we hope it never will.

The following statements are typical of the speeches and writings of A. T. Ariyaratne, founder and president of Sarvodaya Shramadana. The first reading enumerates criticisms of the present social order and contrasts it with the desired order. The ten contrasts are frequently found on posters or plaques on the walls of Sarvodaya buildings in many places in Sri Lanka. The second reading provides a sample of the interesting political thought of Ariyaratne. He discusses political power and non-violence but wishes to avoid political parties. The third reading outlines his reconception of the Buddhist tradition. All of the readings are exerpted from A. T. Ariyaratne, In Search of Development: The Sarvodaya Shramadana Movements Effort to Harmonize Tradition with Change, Moratuwa, Sri Lanka, Sarvodaya Press.

The Desired Sarvodaya Socioeconomic Order

A.T. Ariyaratne

Characteristics of our Present Social Order	Desired Sarvodaya Social Order
1. People's attitude indicates lack of self-knowledge and self-reliance.	1. People strive towards self-realization and self-reliance.
2. People are inclined to blindly follow materialistic values.	2. People are motivated by indigenous cultural and spiritual values; they learn to accept values, etc. on the basis of experience.
3. Worshiping of wealth, power, and position and generally, resorting to untruth, violence, and the achieving of selfish ends are more the rule than the exception.	3. People respect virtue, wisdom, and skills and rely on truth, non-violence, and self-denial.
4. Organizations based on the possessive and competitive instinct become strong. Capitalistic economy, bureaucratic control, power, and party politics have become major social forces.	4. Organizations are based on sharing, and cooperation becomes powerful. People's politics are based on economic trusteeship and people's participation and partyless democracy become social forces.

5.	Evil that is in man is better harnessed. Society gets fragmented into castes and racial, religious, or party-political groups.	5.	Good in man is harnessed. Society tends to get integrated into one human family. All forces that divide people give way to forces that unify them.
6.	Economic resources are indiscriminately exploited. Economy becomes weak. Unemployment increases.	6.	Economic resources are carefully consumed or exploited. Production increases. Employment is assured.
7.	Depends on an import-export economy based on colonial-inherited patterns of production of cash crops. Foreign debts increase.	7.	Ensures a self-sufficient economy based on people's basic needs--an economy not burdened by foreign debts. National self-respect and economic freedom are preserved.
8.	Economy subjugated by large-scale organizations. Human labor lies idle. Corruption is increased. Environment is polluted.	8.	Small-scale organizations are preferred. Labor intensive methods are used. Society is free from corruption. Psychological and environmental pollution do not take place.
9.	Villages subserve the cities. Rural exodus, moral degeneraction, and social unrest result.	9.	Balanced village and urban awakening. Moral reconstruction predominates.
10.	Power of the laws of punishment and the state laws of righteousness and people's power weaken.	10.	Laws of righteousness and the power of the people become strong. No ruling class as such exists. People's power becomes supreme. Sarvodaya ideal is realized.

Present Economic Order in Sri Lanka	Sarvodaya Economic Order
1. Strives to satisfy the unending greed in man.	1. Principal attention is toward the satisfaction of basic human needs.
2. Encourages people to adopt an alien way of life which is patterned after industrialized societies but cannot be sustained by national resources.	2. Attempts to encourage people to adopt a sustainable and simple pattern of life on a foundation of spiritual, moral, and cultural values and social realities.
3. Places faith in large-scale projects, the most modern technology, massive investments of capital, and powerful marketing devices.	3. Puts faith in small-scale projects, socially appropriate technologies, small-scale capital investments, and commercial institutions under people's control.
4. Gives first place to production which brings in a cash income from which need satisfaction is expected; quality of life is measured in quantitative terms.	4. First place is given to production which satisfies needs of people; the quality of life is measured in qualitative terms.
5. Land, labor, capital, and entrepreneurship are considered the basic factors on which development planning is done.	5. Nature, man, society, and scientific knowledge are considered the principal factors on which economic progress is based.
6. Accepts the concept that after a certain age every person should personally receive a private	6. Plans are made on the principle that every human being should participate in efforts to satisfy primarily the

salary or income; plans are made accordingly to generate employment.	basic human needs through righteous means of livelihood.
7. By depending on foreign aid, foreign borrowings, foreign management expertise, foreign technology, and an import-export economic system, the Sri Lanka economy is tied to an international economic network controlled by industrialized countries.	7. Believes in establishing non-dependent relationships with foreign economies and in liberating ours from foreign economic strangle-holds through dependence on self-reliance, national investments, national industries, national creativity, appropriate technologies and attaining national self-sufficiency in basic needs.
8. Allows the benefits of natural and human resources to be drawn away from rural societies to urban and foreign exploitative organizations.	8. Strives to reactivate the rural economy by bringing wealth into rural societies and reinvesting within it the wealth they produce righteously.
9. Makes the human being a confused and restless person caught in a vicious economic cycle.	9. Helps human beings to be contented and composed persons who derive joy from the work they do.
10. Helps a privileged minority to acquire a disproportionate amount of wealth and makes them wasteful, luxury-loving, and playful individuals without a depth in life whilst the majority of people in the country are forced to exist, without even the barest needs, thus making them discontented, frustrated, and angry.	10. Encourages all people in the country to fully satsify their basic needs and build up for themselves a simple, contented, creative, and cultured life.

Sarvodaya and Politics

Sarvodaya theory is inalienably wedded to politics, although it has no relationship with party and power politics as such, Sarvodaya works independently of all political ideologies and excludes all those involved in party politics from having a hand in the formulation of its policy or implementation. Yet Sarvodaya is deeply committed to politics in the sense that it hopes to make people conscious of their rights. This in turn involves the techniques of increasing the participation of the people in the decision-making processes as well as the implementation of decisions made. Sarvodaya hopes to secure the fullest participation of the people in their own affairs and believes in the inalienable goodness of human life and the right of man to enjoy equally and fully all that life can provide. In this sense, one could say that Sarvodaya theory is highly political. But beyond this, Sarvodaya does not hope either in the present or the future to get itself involved in any battle to secure the reins of political power into its hands.

Theoretically, Sarvodaya is committed to dynamic nonviolence. It condemns violence as a means of making social change when there are always nonviolent ways available to achieve these aims. Violence is abhorred because violence always begets violence. Nonviolent revolution is the Sarvodaya ideal. It is called dynamic nonviolence in order to make it clear that it does not mean mere passive disobedience. When human beings are organized, made conscious of their own rights, they can become instruments of active revolution. The revolution Sarvodaya believes in transforms society not by the transference of political, economic, or social power from one party, class, or group to another. It means in the full Sarvodaya sense the transfer of all such power to the people. For this purpose both man and society have to change. The change in the individual has to be reciprocated by a corresponding change in society and vice versa. A mere change in the instrument of power does not bring about the desired transformation of society. In order to transfer political, economic, and social power to all, man has to change. This change comes about by a change in his personality. Man has to awaken in the material as well as the spiritual senses, at the same time awakening also his fellow men or, in other words, society. Once this change is brought about, the immense potential in man is realized, and then the world will be a fitting place to live where all human beings enjoy the best in human life to the fullest capacity.

The Social Philosophy of the Sarvodaya Shramadana Movement

In the Buddhist teachings, as much emphasis had been given to community awakening and community organizational factors as pertain to the awakening of the individual. In the three Refuges a Buddhist accepts next to the Buddha and the Dhamma (doctrine) is the Sangha (the community of monks). Lord Buddha had laid down in great detail the discipline and the organizational principles and forms that the Sangha should adhere to. For the laymen in all matters, the Sangha was the ideal and the example.

During colonial times, particularly during the time of the British rule, many Western scholars overemphasized the view that the Buddhist doctrine was exclusively for the purpose of renunciation of worldly life and that it was primarily an individualist approach to enlightenment. In the absolute sense, this may be true because, when it comes to the final stage of enlightenment, each individual has to strive for himself or herself by one's own efforts and achieve self-realization spiritually. But this fact in no way meant that the conduct and behavior of an individual in the family, in a social group, and in the village or national or universal situation found no place in the teachings of Buddha. The Western powers always attempted to disrupt the unity of the Sangha and to keep them away from the social-political and economic life of the community. Even after independence, many genuine Buddhist leaders feared that the involvement of the Sangha in the affairs of laymen would pollute their spiritual life.

What an unjust ruler feared most was the freedom of the mind that the Buddha advocated.

In the Kalama Sutta Lord Buddha tells the Kalamas,

> Do not accept anything on mere hearsay. Do not accept anything on mere tradition. Do not accept anything on account of rumors. Do not accept anything just because it accords with your scriptures. Do not accept anything by mere supposition. Do not accept anything by merely considering the reasons. Do not accept anything merely because it seems acceptable. Do not accept anything thinking that the ascetic is respected by us.
>
> When you know for yourselves these things are immoral, these things are blameworthy, these things are censured by the wise, these things when performed and undertaken conduce to ruin and sorrow then indeed do you reject them.
>
> When, Kalamas, you know for yourselves these things are moral, these things are blameless, these things are praised by the wise, these things when performed and undertaken conduce to well-being and happiness, then do you live acting accordingly.

These words of the Buddha are like the first charter of the freedom of thought of the human being.

In Buddha's own words in Maha Mangala Sutta, for the happiness and the healthy awakening of the personality of an individual, the environment in which he or she is living (Pathi Rupa Desa Vasa) is emphasized. The Sarvodaya Shramadana Movement has accordingly chosen as its first Basic Human Need "a clean and a beautiful environment." Not only the natural and social environmental factors but also the psychological environment in which one lives is included in the environment we speak of.

In traditional Sri Lankan Society, four factors of social conduct which were meant for the community were held in high esteem. They were Dana or sharing, Priya Vacana or pleasant language, Artha Charya or constructive activity, and Samanathmata or equality in association. These principles were adopted by the Sarvodaya Movement and applied in practical terms in all its multifarious activities.

These four qualities of social conduct could be the guiding factors for small groups, such as the nuclear family, as well as for large groups of human beings, such as those of a village, a nation, or the world community itself.

1. Meet frequently.
2. Meet in unity, discuss in unity, and disperse in unity.
3. Don't impose new laws which are unjust. Don't repeal existing laws which are just. Follow existing just laws.
4. Respect one's elders and listen to them.
5. Respect and protect the females and the weak.
6. Look after those spiritually enlightened persons of the community, and invite such persons from outside also to visit them.
7. Look after and perform those duties that are customary in places of worship.

The above seven factors of nondegeneration were first enunciated by the Buddha when he was preaching to the Vijjins. These seven conventions become the guidelines for any assembly of Buddhists after that. The holding of Sarvodaya Family Gatherings very frequently and almost daily is a revival of the first two conventions. The others too are used to bring about psychological and social integration of the members of the village community.

The teaching of the Buddha, as we have already stated, permeates the entire socioculture, and this has been the pattern for nearly twenty centuries. These teachings were "rediscovered" by

Sarvodaya, not through academic research but by empirical experience. The simple process adopted of going to the rural villagers and working in these areas taught us how, among those rustic folk, these teachings had helped to fashion their way of life. It convinced us how for centuries the socioeconomic structure of the village was modelled on these teachings, not at an abstruse or abstract level but at a very simple empirical level. It is true that one does not find the full implications of the theory permeating rural areas. But there is evidence which shows that these are accepted as practical teachings aimed at improving their way of life. The theoretical framework of Sarvodaya is, in a sense, a rediscovery of a living tradition. In another sense, it is not a rediscovery of a tradition that is dead but a vibrant tradition still conspicuous among many people. The tradition was rediscovered, not by academic research but by going to the people and learning from them.

In the process of building a theory with traditional roots, Sarvodaya laid emphasis on the utility, availability, and feasibility of the theory as concerns the common man for whose welfare it is intended. Utility was beyond doubt, as evident from its presence coming down twenty centuries or more, the while facing tremendous changes in society but surprisingly adapting itself to suit such changes. Availability is not in question because, in every village, almost everyone knows about it, and no special initiation into it was necessary. Feasibility was inherent in it, as the rural folk used the theory and are still using it either in whole or in part. What was necessary was to fuse the entire theory to an active work program, and it is here that the theory was confronted by powerful obstacles.

In the first place, although the theory was there available to everyone, the rural folk somehow have lost sight of the dynamic force which it could generate in meeting today's economic and social problems. Having undergone three centuries or more of foreign rule in which very little encouragement to the dynamic role that such a theory could ignite was made available, they became oblivious to the important role that this theory could play in development. Let us illustrate this by an example. Karma, which we explained above, is now taken to be a pessimistic and unalterable law by the folk, who regard every act or the result of an act as Karma. If one is poor or ill or has to suffer the ignominy of social exploitation, he would very pessimistically ascribe this to Karma. This is due mainly to his failure to understand correctly what Karma means. In building Sarvodaya theory, once the true meaning is uncovered--that Karma is volition and it does not cover every action or result we encounter in this world--the pessimistic attitude to life changes. Inactivity or lethargy suddenly transforms itself into activity leading to social and economic development. Sarvodaya restored the theory from abeyance and fused it to a live program of action which had a meaningful impact on people's lives.

The second obstacle faced by Sarvodaya as far as its theoretical basis was concerned arose from the fact that, because its theory is basically enriched by Buddhist tradition, it had to discover whether it could finally weld itself into a theoretical framework that would motivate the entire nation, which is composed of three or four major ethnic and religious groups. An examination of the foundation of the Sarvodaya theory would show that the entire theory is welded together and geared to further all efforts of man to serve his fellow beings. The four basic levels of loving-kindness, compassionate action, altruistic joy, and equanimity, as well as sharing, pleasant speech, striving for one's own and other's success, and equality, transcend all attempts to categorize them as teachings of a particular group or creed. The empirical philosophy enshrined in them would guide and motivate every human being, irrespective of his caste, creed, or race, to live correctly. Moreover, in rural villages Sarvodaya has observed how for generations people of different ethnic, social, or religious backgrounds merged together, fashioning their ways of life on these principles. In Sri Lanka the theory of Sarvodaya, mainly inspired from Buddhist ideals, had a unique transformation in the hands of the people among whom, bereft of its religious color, it became a common empirical basis for living. Even today, instances can be observed of such rural villages where people of different faiths or ethnic origins carve out their way of life and path of development according to these ideals. Here again Sarvodaya theory has been empirical; that is, it is not a theory extracted from abstract thinking but a theory tested and found existing among the rural folk.

The third obstacle so far as theory is concerned is the accusation advanced by some who say the theory sets an ideal that is impossible to achieve in practice. The simple principles enunciated above are being practiced by many of our villagers. At the time when Sarvodaya pioneers initiated the campaign in the villages, they found how in some remote villages the vestiges of the practice of this theory were still perceptible.

In certain others they were really in practice. The principle of sharing not only their labor but also their harvest has been a cardinal tenet in their lives. Due to the advent of the imperialists and the influx of values that had no relevance to rural life, the practices wedded to such a theory began to disappear. Today, the entire program of Sarvodaya work is carefully formulated in order to make the theory blossom into practice. In spite of obstacles that originate from outside as well as within the village, we find that the theory can be fruitfully translated into practice to a significant extent.

It is argued by some that in a fast-changing world preparing itself briskly for industrialization and modernization, a theory of this nature having its roots in tradition will not have a meaningful role to perform. As the answer to this criticism, Sarvodaya basically accepts that without the understanding of tradition any new theory or program forced upon the people, however innovative or ingenious it may be, will not reap desired results. The tradition of the people has to be the base on which a new theory or program should be introduced.

(From A.T. Ariyaratne, In Search of Development, Moratuwa, Sri Lanka, Sarvodaya Press, 1982, pp. 34-35, 38-39, 51-52, 18-20, 29-31.)

IV

The Christian Workers Fellowship

Beginnings of the Christian Workers Fellowship

The Christian Workers Fellowship of Sri Lanka began in 1978 as a loose association of white-collar workers in the downtown areas of Colombo. At first the group called itself "The Christian Workers Conference." It was a lay movement outside of any formal institutional church structure, nondenominational, but consisting predominantly of Anglicans, Roman Catholics, and Methodists. The majority of the participants were English-speaking Sinhalese.

The social democratic and Marxist movements had developed a number of diverse streams in Sri Lanka by the time the Christian Workers Fellowship formed. These movements often were led by the intelligentsia, persons of cosmopolitan culture who had turned to socialist and Marxist ideas as the most advanced expressions of Western thought. It was natural to them to view leftist movements as critiques of the colonialism that had recently been shed. The CWF identified itself as part of the struggle for a socialistic order, influenced both by Fabian socialism and Trotskyite Marxism that had become important in Sri Lankan politics. Lenski has pointed out that the first manifesto of the Lanka Sama Samaja Party resembled "more the sober Fabian approach than the revolutionary philosophy of the full-blooded Marxists."[1] However, before and during the Second World War a Trotskyite ideology developed. The Christian Workers Fellowship cannot be labeled; it has clearly been anti-Stalinist, and it has published some of Trotsky's writings in its Bulletin (e.g., "A Marxist Vision of the Future", Christian Worker, Bulletin of the Christian Workers Fellowship, Colombo, May Day, 1980). The new organization was responding mainly to the growing trade union movement and unrest among industrial workers in Colombo.

Trade Unionism in Sri Lanka

Trade unions have as long a history of growth in Sri Lanka as in many "developed" countries, and the country has a tradition of campaigns for social justice by trade unions, political groups, and religious bodies. The first unions were formed in the printing trades in 1895; later laundrymen, railway workers and harbor workers were organized. Some of the unions were led by middle-class reformers. Railway and tram workers have been the largest single body of workers.

Justice in the industrial sector has been promulgated by state intervention to redress inequality and inequities. Safety, welfare, workmen's compensation, and maternity benefits have all been addressed by legislation. In the year before the founding of the Christian Workers Fellowship, labor tribunals were established by law to hear complaints from workers and unions.

Purposes of the Fellowship

The original purposes of the Fellowship were twofold: first, "to arouse the consciousness of Christians generally to the need for social action," and second, to encourage Christians already in the work force to align themselves with unions and other working-class organizations.[2] In a statement issued in 1958 the Fellowship asserted "a belief in a social order in which 'material things'--the means of production, distribution and exchange--are used not for the private advantage and profit of a few, but for the common good of all, a society in which no owing and exploiting class stands between the people and their access to these 'things'."[3]

Workers' Masses

During the first years of the organization the "Workers' Mass" was initiated. This mass has become part of May Day celebrations in Sri Lanka. The May Day celebrations, with their significance for political groups and labor unions, had their origin in the violence unleashed on May 1, 1886, in Chicago and a subsequent workers' protest meeting held in Haymarket Square. Seven leaders of the protest were framed and four were eventually hanged. The Socialist International in 1889 declared May 1 a day to celebrate solidarity in remembrance of the Haymarket martyrs. The Sri Lankan May Day Workers' Mass has often been arranged by laymen, with clergy from different Christian denominations concelebrating the Eucharist. The celebration is most often held Sri Lankan-style in the open air, with songs, drama, and readings reflecting the labor and socialist traditions. Two nationally known Christian leaders who have recently died, Lakshman Wickremesinghe, Anglican bishop of Kurunegala, and the Catholic bishop Leo Narayakkara, both exceedingly articulate supporters of workers' causes, frequently presided; Buddhist monks have participated many times. In 1982, May Day was celebrated with a mass and drama at the CWF center in Hatton in the tea plantation country as well as at Ratmalana in Colombo. An earlier tea plantation May Day Workers' Mass included a dialogue sermon led by Anna Abayasekera and Father Paul Casperz. Anna is part of a husband-wife team staffing the Hatton CWF center. Father Casperz is a well-known social critic and Catholic leader.

The Workers' Mass has become a rallying point for the movement--and not just on May Day. The flavor and the complications of the celebration held at Badulla in August, 1981, by a new CWF group were described in the Christian Worker:

> For the first time in Badulla Buddhist monks from three leading Temples in the area attended a Christian Service. . . . The mats used at the Service were lent by the local Mosque, and representatives of the Hindu Temple too were present. A group of young musicians in the area who are Buddhists helped to orchestrate the music as their contribution. The Mass itself was sung in Sinhala to contemporary drama music with portions rendered in Tamil. . . .
>
> The wonderful and inspiring act of witness was however lost on some local middle-class Christians devoid as they normally are of any sense of genuine

> mission. This handful representing "Christian" reaction or more correctly inaction, and who appeared to be led by an aging deacon--a retired State pensioner quite innocent of either theology or liturgy--and a couple of equally unconcerned church members decided to boycott the Service. The Roman Catholic priest expected to join in celebrating the Mass unfortunately failed to turn up and a local roman priest present stood immobile during the celebration. But what is worse, the Sinhalese assistant priest of the Anglican church in Badulla abandoned his Tamil vicar, leaving the latter alone to sing the Worker's Mass in Sinhala to the strains of the drama music provided by the Buddhist musicians.[4]

Perhaps any attempt to be creatively inclusive across lines of religion, language, ethnicity, caste, and class is bound to be complex!

Ecumenical Cooperation

Members of the Fellowship recognized early that if they were to gain the support of industrial workers, they would have to relate to and work with many people who were Buddhist, Hindu, or Muslim, since Christians in Sri Lanka comprise only 7 percent of the populace--perhaps twice that proportion in Colombo. Christians, as in most of Asia, are a distinct minority. If the CWF were to work within the culture, its leaders and members had to appreciate and understand Buddhistic beliefs and practices. The CWF did not set out to be an exclusive association. It very early combined some Buddhist religious elements with Christian ones. By 1978 and the publication of <u>Vandana</u>, it had developed a worship service including a "Buddhist Meditation on Compassion" (<u>Maithri Bhavana</u>) and excerpts from both the Vedas and the Upanishads as well as Sinhala poetry. These were set within a framework of Christian hymns, prayer, and scripture that and concluded with the singing of the "Internationale."

Both in the Vandana and in later Holy Week services, there occurs the Thirsaranaya (the Triple Refuge). However, the CWF version has participants take refuge in the Father, Son, Spirit, and Church rather than in the Buddha, Dharma, and Sangha. (This adaptation is open to some question about its thoughtfulness.) The Workers' Mass and the Holy Week services are creatively specific on the need to remedy economic injustice. In a section entitled "The Sacrament of Repentance", a prayer is made to "empower us to fight fearlessly to end all exploitation and oppression, to overcome unjust social structures."[5] In the "Agape Service" comes a call for "a revolution of mind and spirit, a revolution of social, economic and political, an unceasing revolution in human relationships."[6]

The Easter Eve service at Ratmalana commences with a vigil held outside at dusk. The Red Flag of the workers, "which is identified also with the blood-red banner of the Son of Man," is in the midst of the assemblage. The Paschal Lamp is lighted and carried into the dark building with the Red Flag. The Gospel is proclaimed as candles are lighted. "Christ is risen" is cried to the accompaniment of festive drums.

A section of the Workers' Mass enunciates the vision and purpose of CWF:

> As we in fellowship have shared this food--
> Your gifts and symbols too of mankind's work--
> So may all men for the common good
> Share in all the products of our earth.
> With this manna for our march we go
> Hopefully, joyfully, to serve you more
> In the struggle to free all men
> And in that struggle power to wrest
> For the working people then
> In the interests of all.
> In this way with your grace we can
> Help build a new society, a new man
> A new heaven and a new earth:
> In your strength we now go forth.[7]

The Worker's Mass of the Christian Worker's Fellowship is distinctively Sri Lankan in character, yet it has many interesting roots. The dress of the servers, the use of incense burners of the same type used in Buddhist temple processions, the blowing of the conch shell, the use of drums and music, all are local. The writing of the liturgy was influenced by that of Saint Mark's-in-the-Bouwerie, New York, as well as by Eastern Orthodox rites and the Roman Catholic and Anglican. The mass combines the religious and socio-political themes of the coming of God's Kingdom and the new classless society. The passion of Jesus is clearly viewed as parallelling the struggle of people to liberate themselves from oppression. The celebration of the death and resurrection is the final symbol of liberation. At the conclusion of the mass a Sri Lankan version of the _Internationale_ is sung. Buddhist influence seems to be primarily the _Thirsaranaya_ (the Triple Refuge) mentioned earlier and in the periods of silence occuring at various times during the mass. The clergy leading in the liturgy often come from the Roman Catholic, Anglican and Methodist traditions. Care has been taken to invite Buddhist monks to the masses and to recognize them with places of honor.

The Poson festival, which marks the introduction of Buddhism to Sri Lanka from India by the Arahat Mahinda, is celebrated with open-air drama and festivities at the Christian Workers' Center in Ratmalana. At this center a small statue of Gautama Buddha stands in one meeting room, and Wapola Rahula's well-known work _What the Buddha Taught_ has been used as a study book. The thinking of CWF is further reflected in a description of the place of worship at the branch in Badulla:

> High up on one of its walls is the Arabic text Allahhu Akbar (God is great) with translations in Sinhala and Tamil. Below it is a picture of the crucified Christ (Salvador Dali's Christ of St. John of the Cross) and under this is the altar table for offerings of light (coconut oil lamps), joss sticks and flowers. On the left of this central picture is a picture of an ancient bronze statue of the Buddha found in Badulla in an attitude of discourse (Ministry of the Word) while on

the opposite i.e. right hand side, is a picture of the famous old bronze Nataraja (Dancing Siva) statue found at Polonnaruwa with the communion bowl and plate placed on the table below it (Ministry of the Sacrament).[8]

In 1979 the Christian Workers Fellowship and the Sri Lanka Baudhda Maha Sammelanaya, an important Buddhist outreach organization, jointly published a short book Budu-dharma ha Janatana or Buddhism and the People. The work is addressed to ordinary readers from the working class. It examines the relation between Buddhism and socialism, clarifying and interpreting the basic tenets of socialism in the light of Buddhism. Father Aloysius Pieris, S.J., reviewing this volume in the Lanka Guardian, points out that this is the first work ever published jointly by a Buddhist and a Christian organization. He suggests that "one could sense here a confluence of Christian Radicalism, Marxist Socialism and the aspirations of the Sinhala Buddhist Masses."[9]

Development of the Christian Workers Fellowship

In its growth, the CWF has both responded to social trends and felt the impact of social upheavals. Stages in its development are marked by the founding of new centers and by the expanding of its role in social crises.

The CWF's forerunner, the Christian Workers' Conference, started in 1958, was composed mainly of English-speaking Sinhalese. A 1975 publication looks back upon it as a "petit bourgeois group".[10] The early period witnessed the growth of such religious celebrations as the Workers' Masses, lecture and discussion meetings at the Fort "Y", and the establishment of a downtown office.

According to CWF's own reflections it was not until nine years later, in 1967, that the Fellowship became "involved in a serious study of our social problems".[11] On May Day, 1968, a pamphlet entitled "Social Change in Ceylon" appeared--a first attempt by any Christian group to examine in print the social and economic implications of the Christian faith. After 1967 the CWF made concerted effort to develop its work and publications in Sinhala rather than mainly in English.

The Ratmalana Center

To locate a center near to an industrial area, a new headquarters was established in 1969 in Ratmalana, just north of Colombo. It was to become a major point of contact with workers in railroads, textiles, plastic, shoes, and aluminum products, and workers in smaller factories in the area. The Government Railway Workshop, which employs 6,000 workers, is by far the largest plant. Women workers predominate in some of the smaller clothing and food-processing establishments.

A wide-ranging program was to develop at the Ratmalana Center. Worker education classes on economics, employee rights, radical issues, and social action have become regular activities. A very popular preschool opened in 1982 with forty children, has provided effective links with workers' families. English classes, sewing classes, and a drama group are conducted by the center. All these activities are enhanced by a new program building finished in the fall of 1981. "Pirith" was chanted by monks of the nearby Buddhist Vihara and prayers said by Christian clergy to dedicate the building on October 24, 1981. Nowadays, members discussing plans for Holy Week services in the second-floor offices may overhear an informal talk on economics in the upstairs classroom or the sounds of Brecht being rehearsed in Sinhalese next door. (Brecht seems to be a favorite with the drama group, and his writings are occasionally excerpted in the _Christian Worker_. _Mother Courage_,

Calk, and The Three Penny Opera have all been performed in Sinhalese.)

The Christian Workers Fellowship and its Ratmalana Center were deeply affected by a traumatic national insurrection instigated by the Marxist party, Jathika Vimukti Peramuma (JVP), in 1971. This insurrection was remarkable because it was the first one by a political party composed mainly of young people seeking to change society by revolutionary violence. The underlying causes of the upheaval were widespread unemployment, the failure of the educational system to focus on the economic and functional needs of the society, and rapid population growth, which excaberated the problems of unemployment and schooling. The real breakthrough in the movement came when the JVP was able to recruit university students who could provide leadership.

The actual violence of the insurrection involved an active group of about 10,000, with perhaps 70,000 others in support roles. A high proportion of the 16,355 taken prisoner by the government had had some secondary education.

Many groups with dissident views were suspect. The Christian Workers Office in downtown Colombo was sealed by the police for two days. Sometime later the organization sent a letter to the prime minister recommending amnesty for those in prison. The uprising shocked the nation into awareness of the alienation and despair of many of its youth. The 1971 CWF May Day Mass held at the height of the emergency was by all reports a particularly moving one.

The Fellowship assisted some of those in jail. Among the people it befriended was a student, Kingsley Perra, who served a year in prison. During his incarceration he read books by Dietrich Bonhoeffer and other Christian thinkers and had a profound religious experience. After his release he began working with the CWF; now he directs the Ratmalana Center.

A more recent crisis involving the Ratmalana Center was the railway workers' strike and lockout of 1980. On July 7 twelve railway workers were dismissed, after taking time off to attend the funeral of a trade union leader killed by thugs during a picketing march. The railway workers went on strike to protest the dismissal, and others joined in. As a result the government dismissed an estimated 100.000 workers. The CWF participated in a country-wide appeal by religious groups to the government for justice. Under the leadership of Father Lionel Peiris the CWF established a Lockout Victims' Fund and sold tea in the Ratmalana neighborhood to raise funds for welfare activities during the lockout.

Protest activities continued into early 1982 before remedial action was haltingly taken by the government. The Ratmalana Center was one of several sites where a trade union protest fast was conducted for three days at the end of January of that year.

The Hatton Center

An explosion of racial tension into violence led to the establishment of a CWF Center in Hatton in the tea plantation country of Sri Lanka in August of 1977. The conflict stemmed from the resentment of Sinhala people in the Kandyan area toward tea workers of Indian origin, mainly Tamils. A stagnant economy intensified Sinhalese fear of the growing "foreign population" that was competing for the few available jobs.

Tea plantations and tea workers constitute a distinct and important segment of Sri Lankan economy and life. The British government had expropriated the central highlands of Sri Lanka to establish tea plantations and had thereby disrupted the village agricultural culture. Between 1823 and 1886 the British sold over a million acres of this land to British planters for tea and coffee plantations.[12] In traditional Sinhala society in the highland areas, landholdings generally included a section of rice paddy land in a valley, a section of highland, and a home and garden in a village. The peasant farmer would work his paddy and his highland holdings at a distance from his dwelling. The highland provided pasture and fodder and yielded pulses and some cereal crops. Firewood and timber were sometimes also grown there.

The British brought an export-oriented plantation economy that weakened and in many areas destroyed the traditional subsistence agriculture of the peasants. The imported Tamil laborers, ethnically distinct and locked into a semicaptive labor market, cannot become citizens and so do not have voting rights. Outbreaks of violence between them and Sinhalese have not been uncommon.

The 1977 eruption affected a number of areas of the country, and plantation workers experienced massive suffering. Over a hundred died, and thousands were left homeless.

In response, in August of 1977, a group of plantation workers, teachers, and others from the community met in Hatton to organize a center of the Christian Workers Fellowship. Hatton is a strategic center in the tea country because many tea workers' unions have their headquarters there. The property used by the CWF was given by the Methodist Church.

Jeffrey and Annathgail Abayasekera have been the directors of the Hatton Center since 1977. Jeffrey had served as treasurer of his trade union and helped organize a Christian cell while working at the Central Bank in Colombo. Later he became a member of the Christian monastic community known as Devasaranaramaya--a group active in peasant rights activities, land reform, and interreligious understanding. Anna was president of the Student Christian Movement in Sri Lanka.

The work of the center has several aspects. First, it has organized CWF plantation worker groups--six to nine of them--over the last few years. These groups serve as the base for leadership training camps, drama workshops, health training seminars, and other worker education activities. On some plantations a small library also has been established.

Anna has given leadership in education for women tea pluckers. Nutrition and family health care are crucial dimensions for women workers because government services in these areas rarely extend to plantation areas. The focus on the role and identity of women workers, who are paid less than men and who are more bound by the traditional patterns of Hindu culture, is unique to CWF educational efforts on the plantations.

Musical training and encouragement of Tamil cultural programs is another focus of CWF educational work. A group of Tamil writings reflecting the experience of plantation workers themselves was published in 1978. To communicate these experiences to other groups, a translation of these writings was then put into Sinhala and English. The Christian Conference of Asia published some of these in 1981.[13]

Because Hatton is the center for many tea workers' unions, CWF is in a strategic position to work with the unions. It has helped sensitize the unions to plantation problems and workers' needs and served as a support group in such crises as strikes. Jeffrey Abayasekera has been elected convenor of the Hatton Joint Committee of Trade Unions and Voluntary Organizations. In December of 1982, while preparing to visit some plantations with union leaders to recruit observers for balloting during the parliamentary election, he was beaten by thugs apparently inspired by the party of the national administration. He and two union leaders were jailed overnight, in spite of the fact that no charge was made against them.

CWF is one of the few organizations that seeks to link the difficult plight of tea plantation workers, rural peasant farmers, and industrial workers in Colombo. The linking is done through shared leadership training, visits of worker groups to other areas, islandwide celebrations and masses, and the bringing in of resource persons from different areas for special programs. (Because Sri Lanka is not a large island, such activities are not difficult to arrange.) Recently, the Hatton Center has also had an exchange program with Malaysian rubber workers. One plantation worker was sent to India for a three-week training seminar.

The tea plantation workers face a particularly trying struggle for a fuller humanity. The goals of CWF on the plantaions are for a just wage (men earn sixteen rupees a day, women fourteen--less than a dollar), equal health and educational services, the opportunity to own land, and the right to use their own language in official matters.

A poem written by a plantation worker from the CWF collection of writings cited earlier reveals the aspirations of the tea workers.

The New Woman[14]

The hands which gently tend the leaves
Will now help to banish darkness;
They'll work hard to put down evil,
And to raise up for all new life.

The hands which gently tend the leaves
Will help nourish all that is good;
They'll work hard to weed poverty
And bring in new culture and art.

The hands which gently tend the leaves
Will show men ways for humankind;
They'll work hard to build those structures
In which truth and right will be found.

Kurinji Nathan

The Galaha Center

In June of 1977 the CWF founded a center and farm at Galaha, a small farming community fourteen miles west of Kandy in the central section of Sri Lanka.

By 1980 the farm had sixteen milk cows, rabbits, goats poultry for egg production, and vegetable gardens. The farm, located on a hillside of eroded former tea land, is planted with a variety of grasses to remedy the erosion problem and serve as pastureland. The farm is worked by ten persons who are experimenting with fertilizers. Construction has been completed on a biogas tank, which makes gas from pig manure for cooking and heating water. A residence for about six persons is part of the farm.

The nearby center is a small one-story building astride the main road at the top of the hill just above the farm. Here are rooms for children's activities, a small library, offices, and meetingrooms. The goals of the center have been to create self-reliant forms of community economic activity and to foster community cooperation. Both the center and the farm provide economic development education.

The most successful effort has been the nurturing of a milk cooperative, now an autonomous village organization still headquartered in the center office. The cooperative, with more than forty farm families, serves seven villages. The members do their own milk collecting, testing, and selling. The co-op has increased the income of the participants and allowed for more efficient and economical purchase of feed supplements for the farmers. Through CWF initiative in 1982-83, the co-op had a volunteer veterinarian to provide essential services and train "barefoot vets" for rural areas. The milk cooperative demonstrates the power of a participatory approach to economic problems, eliminates the middleman, and has enabled the farmers to deal directly with the government milk board. Now the government provides assistance, and officers of the milk board seem enthusiastic about spreading the method to other villages. All of this is part of the larger goal of "conscientizing", promoting a sense of empowerment, and furthering economic and political analysis and dialogue.

Janith De Silva, a former bank auditor and political activist in Colombo, is the director of the Galaha Center. His business training has been a major help to the success of the milk cooperative. Careful and honest records that are open to all members increase their confidence in their ability to control their own lives. The farmers formerly had to depend on the middleman's interpretation of milk analyses and his financial records. Through the milk cooperative in the first year of operation, farmers received an increase of one rupee per liter of milk over the previous price and paid two and a half rupees less for a five pound sack of feed concentrates.

The CWF has observed that the attempts of leftist political parties to build up peasant organizations in Sri Lanka have not succeeded, largely because ideology cast in theoretical terms from above tends to become sterile and meaningless in village settings. CWF has therefore tried to involve itself in a "clear demonstration in practice of the superiority of measures advanced".[15] It has combined village projects, demonstrations of improved agriculture, and cooperative production with broader economic and political analysis--an important combination, but one difficult to keep in balance. Leaders in one areas--for example, in agricultural improvement--may not be effective in macro-political analysis, and vice versa. Many areas are subject to national decisions or international market forces. For example, a rise in oil prices may put small motors out of use and halt the use of petroleum-based fertilizers. The prices of cattle feed and poultry feed go up largely because of national market conditions. Empowering farmers to change what they can at the local level and to understand their political responsibility at the macrolevel is not simple.

Common to farmers in most sections of Sri Lanka are two major problems: (1) Despite some efforts on the government's part at land reform, the sharecropping system that has come down from the past, especially in rice paddy areas, is a barrier to improved production. (2) The absence of an organized marketing system leaves cultivators in many areas to the exploitation of traders and middlemen. Because the country is predominantly rural, these two problems are urgent national ones that CWF attempts to treat not only through the political and economic macroanalysis, but also at the more local level, particularly in Galaha, with study and demonstration. The Christian Workers Fellowship is convinced that solutions to the country's rural and agricultural problems cannot be achieved within the capitalist framework. It recognizes, however, that since the assumption of power by the present government in 1977, any effective movement contrary to the government's policy of dependence on foreign capital, capital-intensive agriculture or industrialization, and export-oriented agriculture will have to be built from the grass roots. And building a socialist society from the grass roots requires that rural workers learn self-reliance and awareness of alternatives to middlemen or traders by seeing demonstrations of realistic alternatives. The landless poor will be served not only through more efficient land reform but also through a local structure that encourages food production for local consumption. Effective action toward self-reliance, however, cannot be separated from participation in political parties and linkage to other movements. The Fellowship sees itself as a catalyst in its interactions with other religious and activist oranizations. It maintains strong positions on socioeconomic issues but is not tied to any political party.

It is noteworthy that the Christian Workers Fellowship has worked at integrating and applying distinctively Asian and Christian concepts as its motivating and guiding ethos. The late Bishop Wickremesinghe, one of the founders and leading members of the movement, has dramatically stated the Christian option in Asia:

> The option we Christians have to make in the conflict between the two ideologies (i.e. capitalism and socialism) in our situation has to be shaped by our Christian vision. . . . My own conviction is that the Church must opt for the ideology, programme and strategy covered by the term 'indigenous Marxist socialism'. This is because indigenous

welfare capitalism has been shown incapable of preventing the concentration of profit, power and privilege in dominant groups whereby enhanced growth for some is at the expense of sharing for all.

What implications have all this for us Christians who seek to give theological legitimacy to this ideology, which I call 'indigenous Marxian socialism'? It means giving concrete priority to the image of Jesus as prophetic contestant and martyr. But we are also constrained to hold his image in dialectical tension with the images of Jesus as companion and rehabilitator of sinners and outcasts, and also as the self-sacrificing satyagrahi converting enemies with the soul force of vicarious suffering love. Mao Tse-Tung reminds us that correct ideas or views come from social practice, and we must not forget this. . . . We must be aware of how theory and practice condition each other.[16]

"Spirituality in Combat" is a statement drawn up collectively by the staff of the Christian Workers Fellowship. Most of their writings and many of the editorials in their journal _The Christian Worker_ are group products and have no single author. Evident in this document are CWF's differences with Sarvodaya and with the present Sri Lankan government. Sarvodaya is guilty of supporting the present neocolonial model of development and the government uses Buddhist symbols to legitimize rule concentrated in the hands of a small ruling elite. The goal of liberation through a socialist order will come through struggle and conflict with oppressive power.

SPIRITUALITY IN COMBAT

(A SRI LANKAN REFLECTION)

by the staff of the
Christian Workers Fellowship
1983

1. Definition of Terms

Spirituality means to us a consciousness of the mind and a commitment of the heart and body which has transforming power, in persons and in communities. To us as Christians it describes a total human response under the inspiration and dominion of the Holy Spirit to the in-breaking of the Kingdom of God.

Combat represents to us the reality of our struggle against all forms of evil in a world which has largely rejected the values of the righteous rule of God. Faith, hope, and universal love (our spirituality) can only be concretely expressed through solidarity with the oppressed masses, social and political struggle, conflict and confrontation.

2. Sri Lankan Contest Today

(a) Political

The presidential system of government and the power of the executive president have been consolidated. This has resulted in a devaluation of Parliament, a loss of the people's sovereignty as affirmed by the Republican Constitution of 1972, and the concentration of power in the hands of a small ruling elite. Repressive laws, chiefly the Essential Public Services Act and the Prevention of Terrorism Act, have incorporated features of emergency rule into the normal law of the land. There has been a consolidation of the power of the armed forces and police, and the use of paramilitary forces and thugs to suppress the struggles of the oppressed and to disrupt political meetings is becoming all too common. Successive amendments to the Constitution have been rushed through

Parliament, and the latest amendment has brought forward the presidential election by two years in order to eliminate the political opposition and ensure the stability of the ruling elite for the next decade. The repression of trade unions and workers who went on a general strike in July 1980 continues. The oppression of the Tamil ethnic minorities in the North and the East and in the hill country areas has been underlined by three outbursts of racial violence in 1977, 1980, and 1981, and the demand for a separate state by Tamils in the North and East has been met by severe state repression.

(b) Economic

Our present-day open economy and export-oriented model of development have brought Sri Lanka firmly under the control of monopoly capital and the transnational corporations. Galloping inflation was estimated in 1981 to be 35 percent, but the actual rate is considered to be 45 percent. There has been a massive cutback on subsidies and welfare expenditure in the name of "development." At the same time, heavy "tax expenditures" have been introduced through a system of massive relief measures, tax holidays, accelerated write-offs for capital assets, investment allowances, and exemptions for the benefit of the richer classes under the smokescreen of "development." The economy is obviously geared to benefit the 2 percent in the upper crust of our society, while the oppressed masses groan under the weight of an ever-increasing cost of living. We are precariously in debt as a nation. Our public debt now matches our G.N.P. Deficit budgeting has been the most significant feature of our economic policy. The unbalanced budget of 1982 had a record deficit of Rs.21.1 billion, to be bridged by Rs.4 billion in proposed domestic loans and Rs.14.2 billion in foreign loans and a further Rs.5 million in Treasury bills, leaving an unfinanced deficit of Rs.2.9 billion.

(c) Cultural

This is a period in our history when cultural bondage and the abdication of self-determination under subjection to neo-colonialism are clearly apparent. The control of information is ensured by the state monopoly of television, radio, and the leading newspapers. The rapid spread of western consumerist values is fueled by tourism, the advertising of transnational corporations, television programmes, etc. Alien values and life styles are also imported by our returning migrant workers. These values are in conflict with our own traditional values, which appear to be in disintegration in many areas under the impact of an accelerated modernization process. The repression and control of creative artists engaged in the cultural sphere is also very much in evidence.

(d) Religious

The state patronage afforded to Buddhism is seen in the restoration of Buddhist monuments and places of worship, the updating of the Mahavamsa, the restoration of the Dutugemunu cult, etc. A conscious attempt is made by the rulers to justify the present system through the use of Buddhist religious concepts--e.g., dharmista (righteous). At a recent Human Rights Seminar an attempt was made to utilize religion to underplay human rights violations in our country. Open support is given by the government to institutions like Sarvodaya espousing a Buddhist-Ghandhian ideology which is supportive of the present model of development. Some religious leaders have been coopted with privileges extended to them and foreign trips offered, and they are persuaded to make public statements in times of crisis to support the policies of the government. However, certain Christian clergy who were critical of the government at a recent meeting of the Civil Rights Movement were upbraided by the president of Sri Lanka at a public meeting.

3. Faith Reflections in Our Context

Concrete involvement in the struggles of the oppressed in Sri Lanka leads to the following perspectives:

(a) A strong critique and rejection of the capitalist neocolonial model of development and the counterposing of an alternative indigenous socialist reconstruction society.

Third world countries and all men and women of good will oppose capitalism because it creates a social environment that is unsuitable objectively for the realization of the spiritual growth of peoples. Capitalism breeds greed, inequality, elitism, injustice, arrogance, consumerism, waste, ostentation, unconcern for others, or a mere paternalistic charity. Today it heightens inequalities and imbalances and the exploitation of persons for profit, power, and pleasure. This environment brutalizes human beings, makes them highly civilized barbarians, and destroys human solidarity. Hunger, famine, and unemployment are phenomena of capitalist society. Such a situation is in itself unsuitable for the flowering of human persons in truth, love, justice, equality, and freedom. Individuals may attain spiritual heights in spite of this current, but the whole social environment remains polluted and vitiated. It dehumanizes the affluent and debases the indigent. The structures of society in religion, education, health, etc. as they are presently constituted in most third-world countries continually influence values and relationships in an undesirable way and, instead of combatting forces of capitalism, encourages and sustains these forces.

As opposed to capitalism, the trend in most third-world countries is to drift or, may I say, make a clear option in favour of socialism. Socialism sets out to provide an environment of sharing and concern for the fundamental needs of all. It insists on hard work and provides work for all by a planned use of all available resources. The socialist reorganization of society leaves less room for the accumulation of wealth by a few through the exploitation of others. Many fear and oppose socialistic measures, not because they value spiritual growth or even freedom, but because they do not like to part with their wealth and their privileges. "From each according to his ability, to each according to his needs" is the policy. A socialist society is one that is difficult to live in for those accustomed to affluence, but it is an opportunity for the poor and the oppressed to overcome the evils of unemployment, starvation, malnutrition, ignorance, inequality, and hence, unfreedom. For both the rich and the poor, socialism provides a better public environment of respect for persons and their needs.

From the above analysis, we conclude that it is the principles and social structures of capitalism that all spiritual-minded persons should combat--greed (which is a vice) springs from the policy of selfish profit maximization, which encourages other vices such as consumerism, ostentation, commercialization of sex, leisure, art, etc.

--Sister Pauline

(b) The goal of a socialist society along with the strategies and tactics to move in that direction constitute a new and alternative consciousness springing from the oppression and sufferings of the poor (victims of the dominant classes). Such a consciousness is a dynamic interaction between the experienced oppression and articulation of the poor and the compassion, commitment, and scientific analysis of agents of change (organizers, animators, etc.).

(c) The goal, strategies, and tactics mentioned above must necessarily be judged and nourished by our ultimate vision of the future.

From a Christian position, the ultimate vision would transcend the changes and transformations on the purely political, economic, and social levels. It would be a vision of the Kingdom of God--the classless society of the future and the new age in Christ when God will be all in all. The Christian Workers Fellowship of Sri Lanka at the conclusion of its Workers' Mass expresses its vision of the future and the struggles toward it in the following chant:

We have made memorial of your death O Christ
Your Resurrection's symbol we have seen
Now filled with your undying life
In this Sacrament we have been
United to you and one another.
As we in fellowship have shared this Food--
Your gifts and symbols too of mankind's work
So may all men for the common good
Share in all the products of our earth!
With this manna for our march we go
Hopefully, joyfully to serve you more
In the struggles to free all men
And in that struggle power to wrest
For the working people then
In the interests of all.

In this way by your grace we can
Help build a new society, a new man
A new heaven and a new earth
In your strength we now go forth.

(d) We believe that such a consciousness can emerge within a community life--a "workers fellowship" where the oppressed truly feel a deep sense of belonging and are enabled to share and participate fully, where they "meet constantly to hear the apostles teach, and to share the common life, to break bread and to pray" (Acts 2:42). It is only in such a community that the revolutionary subversive vision can be nourished, the signs of the times discerned in corporate theological reflection and political analysis held together, and the commitment and motivation to bear tensions and suffering within conflictual situations sustained. "Hear the apostles teach" has to be translated in our context today on these lines: "Share experiences and insights of a common ministry in a plural, religious and ideological context."

(e) Thus we see the emergence of open, venturesome communities of faith transcending narrow faith and ideological barriers (transreligio-ideological communities). These action groups and people's organizations committed to human liberation have some if not all of the following characteristics:

(1) Ability to recognize the fruits of the Spirit in other action groups, regardless of whether such groups profess the Christian faith or are of other religious beliefs or secular persuasions (Acts 10:34-35; Acts 10:44-48; Luke 13:24-30; Matt. 21:43).

(2) A prophetic perspective reflecting a counter to the dominant ideology; an ideological stance based on the aspirations of the "have-nots" and backed by a structural analysis of society and an understanding of social classes. The prophetic and the scientific are combined in a single commitment.

(3) Cooperation with other action groups having a common ideological approach. The formation of coalitions or networks leading to broad political actions.

(4) Building awareness of the oppressed linked to the growth of strong people's organizations at the grass-roots level. Micro and macro levels of analysis and organizations around vital issues are a common feature. The people participate fully in all aspects of the life of the group.

(5) Worship which springs from our country's cultural context and reflects proletarian socialist aspirations and is therefore meaningful to people of other faiths and those involved in mass activity. Essential elements of such worship would be silent contemplation or meditation, criticism, self-criticism and experiencing forgiveness, joyful celebration (including songs and dances of devotion), a common meal, and a renewal of strength, commitment and solidarity in the struggle (e.g., the Workers' Mass of the C.W.F., which is open to people of all faiths, celebrated on April 30 every year as a preparation

for May Day and on the first Saturday in May in the plantation areas; also the C.W.F.'s Fellowship Meal [Agape] more suitable for close-knit family groupings, and the New World Liturgy of the Devasarana Development Centre). It is the Spirit that sets free and leads us into all truth on the path to total liberation; hence in worship we lay ourselves open to the power of the Spirit leading our hearts and minds to new levels of awareness, new sensitivities, and an openness to a new future.

(6) A critical spirit that will not seek to absolutize any given economic or political structure. Having a clear ideological stance but one that is open-ended in the service of full humanity. As the C.W.F. says: "Socialism is for Man, not Man for Sociaism". As a "new community," it lives as a ferment and foretaste of the righteous rule of God.

4. <u>Combat Experiences</u>

(a) The Workers' Mass held by the C.W.F. on September 8, 1980, with the special intention of "justice to the workers and an end to the lockout" in the midst of severe repression by the government on workers who participated in the general strike of July 1980, was a national event of great political significance.

This mass was not some form of escapism but an action intimately connected with our struggle and helping to give the struggle its full depth of meaning. After the first part of the Mass--the Service of the Word, at which the Bishop preached, there followed the Ministry of the Sacrament. The offertory procession to the Altar led by the incense bearers had workers' children carrying lotus flowers to offer, followed by the Red Flag and the symbol of working people's labor--bread and wine. Through these symbols we offered the life and toil, the sweat and pain of the workers, their hopes and aspirations, the trade union movement, and the struggle we were facing together with the uncertain future. Then after the Thanksgiving--the Eucharistic Prayer--sung responsively by clergy and people to Sinhala drama music, we had the solemn "breaking of bread" when we were reminded that just as Christ's Body was broken on the cross for us, so we must be ready to be broken for others. Then our eyes were opened: we realized that the bodies of the workers now broken in struggle were in fact a part of Christ's own body broken for the liberation of mankind. Our struggle, pain, and suffering then had a redemptive meaning, for it was all part of the common struggle for human liberation against all oppression and evil, against the rulers of darkness in our society, and against all the demonic forces of the old order. In all this deep symbolism we realized more clearly than ever before that if we wanted to build the new society, we could not do so without sacrifice, without suffering, without facing up to a struggle and a conflict. Yes, now the sufferings of the victimized workers had meaning, had value, and the "breaking of the bread" in this way become a challenge to all.

(b) A Mid-Day Fast to obtain justice for strikers, to provide relief to locked-out workers and their families, and to safeguard basic trade union and democratic rights and freedoms was held on November 11, 1980, at the Sri Sumanaramaya Buddhist Temple, Hatton. A series of meditations were led by leaders of trade unions and voluntary groups (Buddhists, Hindus, and Christians) and also by a Christian clergyman and the chief Buddhist monk of the Temple. Two efforts had been made by the police to ask the chief monk to call this off, but these efforts failed. The unity and determination of those who gathered was strengthened through this fast for justice, and a collection was made for locked-out workers and their families. The interaction of Buddhist, Hindu, Christian, and Marxist thinking was deeply inspiring.

(c) Plantation workers and locked-out workers joined in a celebration of the Workers' Mass on October 22, 1981, in Kandy--the day when the Fiftieth Anniversary of Universal Adult

Franchise was celebrated on a lavish scale in Colombo with the Queen of England present. At this Mass we exposed the injustice done to the plantation workers and to the strikers due to bad legislation and emergency regulations. This Fiftieth Anniversary was brought under the judgment of the Jewish Jubilee Year and the rule of God operative today.

(d) On September 9, 1982, over 750 peasants supported by hundreds of urban-industrial workers, members of voluntary groups, and about 50 plantation workers converged on Colombo to deliver a petition incorporating nine demands to the president of Sri Lanka. In the vanguard of their procession were Buddhist monks and Christian clergy chanting religious texts in Sinhala, with the people responding in traditional style. The police obstructed the procession, and a dialogue among religious leaders, peasant leaders, and the police officers took place on the street. Ultimately, eight leaders were allowed to go to meet the president, but he did not have the courtesy to wait for them; hence the petition with thousands of signatures was presented to his secretary. Meanwhile, for about one hour, a very effective demonstration was held on the street, with posters being displayed and slogans being shouted to create public awareness in regard to the peasants' demands. Hundreds of Colombo workers and passers-by in vehicles witnessed this event. Later the peasant-worker combined force regrouped at De Mel Park, Kompannaveediya, for a public meeting at which peasant leaders, trade union leaders, Buddhist monks, and Bishop Lakshman Wickremesinghe spoke. It was a historic event bringing together six peasant organizations, several trade unions, action groups, and Buddhist and Christian clergy.

V

THAI INTERRELIGIOUS COMMISSION ON DEVELOPMENT

Changes in Thai Society

Thai society has gone through a number of social and economic changes in the last several decades. However, during this period of rapid transition the traditional symbols of nation, monarchy, and religion have provided a focus for national loyalty. Strong, modernizing monarchs such as Mongkut (r. 1851-1868) and Chulalongkorn (r.1868-1910) had secured stability for increasing central authority, rationalizing the bureaucracy, and giving the Sangha a recognized role in the society.

The establishment of a Supreme Ecclesiastical Council (_Mahathera Samakhon_) headed by a supreme patriarch (_Somdet Phrasangkharaat_) in the Sangha Act of 1941 and its 1963 revision has now concentrated ecclesiastical authority and power.[1] Attempts at religious reform, particularly movements within the Sangha critical of the status quo in Thai society, face considerable difficulty. The legitimating and conserving aspects of the Supreme Council may deter criticism. If so, the reform movements we mention may have greater significance than they would if the Sangha hierarchy were less constrictive.

Economically, Thailand has shown real aggregate growth since 1945. After World War II Thailand hastened to implement economic development plans following western patterns, with the result that the urban and industrial sectors grew at the expense of the rural sector and to the detriment of such natural resources as forests. Equitable distribution of income was secondary to investment profit and aggregate growth. However, in the 1950s and 1960s the population also grew at the rate of approximately 3 percent a year. By the 1970s this growth put enormous pressure on the rural population for land. Traditionally, rice growing has been a preferred occupation for many

Thais; even now, it is the major work of 75 percent of the Thai rural population . An old expression, "In the water there are fish; in the fields there is rice" (Nai nam mi pla, nai na mi khao), encapsulates the sense of the abundant life in traditional Thai society, when prosperity meant growing enough rice for the family and finding fish in flooded rice paddies or streams. With the growth of the rural population and the burgeoning of industrial development in Bangkok, migration to the city swelled it beyond its capacity to provide employment or basic human services. The beautiful klongs (canals) have been filled in or polluted; squatter slums huddle in the shadow of air-conditioned concrete monoliths; and tourism for sex is promoted as a growth industry. The greatest economic pressure is on the poorest sections of the country, the northeastern and southern provinces. These are the areas with the greatest increase in political and economic conflict.

The rise of an urban middle class and the growth of a student population brought a number of new complications to a traditionally two-class society. In 1973 a student uprising brought a short-lived period of reform and democracy. Then the military, in cooperation with the growing government bureaucracy, reestablished firm control of the country. In 1976 a student demonstration at Thammasat University was put down with military violence. Between fifty and a hundred students were killed, several hundred were wounded, and three thousand were arrested in what appears to have been unprovoked military repression.[2] Unknown numbers of Thai intellectuals and students fled into exile in the jungle after this violent incident. The repression apparently increased the ranks of communist insurgents, and the student movement became fragmented and demoralized.

In November of 1974, after a number of monks had made an appearance in support of a former demonstrator in Bangkok, the Sangha Supreme Council condemned them. Tension in the Sangha became public when in January, 1975, a thousand monks gathered at Wat Mahaṭat in the center of Bangkok to protest the expulsion of two monks who had been expelled, ostensibly for communist affiliation and sexual misconduct. After a hunger strike by several of the protesters, the accused monks were declared innocent.

The resilience of Thai society in the face of continued military domination and central control is remarkable. One evidence of this resiliency is the growth of groups, some very small, interested in social and economic development, particularly rural development. Many of these groups have formed since 1976. The ones that are religious in nature respond to the alienation of people from the negative effects of bureaucracy and mass movements as well as the negative effects of the imposition of western competitive materialism.

The Thai Interreligious Commission on Development

One group responding to the need for religious and economic renewal is the Thai Interreligious Commission on Development. It is chaired by Phra Pattaramuni, a Buddhist monk. Its executive committee and advisers include two Catholics, the students that comprise the active participants and officers are mostly Buddhist. The Catholic Council on Thai Development has supported the organization, and its chief staff person serves as vice-chairman of T.I.C.D.

The Commission's main efforts are seminars, training programs, and staff support for Buddhist monks who are local village or urban leaders and who are interested in enhancing their role as change agents. T.I.C.D tries to help such leaders to become aware of, analyze, and attempt to solve their problems at the local level. T.I.C.D also conducts its own modest research into development problems and issues as well as into the religious resources of the Thai tradition for handling these problems. Its program promotes understanding "society in its wider context as well as knowledge and know-how at the level that will benefit local monks, such as basic knowledge of public health and medical care, appropriate technology and presentation of art heritage."[3] The Commission also supports low-cost projects in village development and helps solicit support from other agencies for more costly projects.

One of the most interesting religious tasks it has set itself is to encourage young people to "modify and improve their respective religious ceremonies so as to make them up-to-date and in harmony with social conditions that have changed."[4] The intent in such modifications is to enhance the understanding between the rich and the poor, the urban middle class and the rural peasant, the landowner and the landless. (One such reinterpretation is the rice Phapa ceremony, to be described later in this chapter.)

T.I.C.D. also attempts to encourage Buddhist student associations at Thammasat and Chulalongkorn universities to participate in social-service and social-change programs. In 1982-83 it sponsored a study group on the thought of Buddhadasa Bhikkhu, a leading Buddhist monk who has developed an articulate social philosophy. The students involved in T.I.C.D. are convinced that Buddhadasa's is one of the few Buddhist voices in Thailand that appeals to young people. His social and religious criticism is probably the source of his appeal.

In many ways T.I.C.D. attempts to serve as a bridge--between generations, between rural and urban groups, and between religious leaders; it encourages all of these to confront social and economic issues in Thai life. It brings together monks and religious leaders to analyze such problems as rural poverty and to build a problem-solving consciousness. As a religious movement, it also attempts to bridge Buddhist and Christian interests.

In Bangkok, T.I.C.D. has cooperated with other organizations in short-term educational and recreational projects for children in slum areas. It has an ongoing research-and-action project interviewing Buddhist abbots at urban wats to identify the needs and problems they perceive.

Buddhist Wats

The Buddhist wat has its natural habitat in the village. The traditional alms round each morning takes quite a different form in Bangkok, where young monks wander among downtown business buildings and hotels. The abbot's traditional village role was largely related to the agricultural cycle. Abbots and monks in rural areas sometimes participate in "animistic" rituals, either incorporated into a Buddhist context or perhaps without particular Buddhist significance.[5] The rural wat often served as bank, drug store, and hostel. These functions are diminished or lost in Bangkok and other urban centers, although innumerable rituals, festivities, and holidays are still observed.[6]

What are now wats in the bustle of the city of Bangkok were once country places where families went to picnic and to visit with the abbot or monks. Monks who migrated to the city, in times past and even now, are able to support relatives or friends coming to the city. The traditional view, still held by many, is that the wat serves as the father in society and that the children should go to the father, not the father to the children. Several leaders at the World Fellowship of Buddhist Headquarters and some abbots have confirmed this view.[7] While many wats still serve the traditional functions, few of the the wats in Bangkok, Chiang Mai, and other urbanized areas have proposed creative approaches to such issues as slums, high unemployment, pollution, and prostitution. Migrants to Bangkok drop their religious practices markedly, even below the standards of long-time city dwellers.[8] In traditional society, and even today in rural areas, the wat has served as the village school and as a refuge for homeless elderly men. In Bangkok some Buddhist wats serve as residences for bright, young country monks studying at the Buddhist universities. (Study in Bangkok is a useful path to upward mobility for those from the northeast and other poor sections of the nation.)

Some wats in Bangkok own and rent the land surrounding them. Indeed, profit from such undertakings, for whatever purpose, is not uncommon. Some slum property is owned and controlled by Bangkok wats.[9] T.I.C.D. has begun to tackle some of these issues in a study of the concerns and problems of urban abbots.

The Phapa Ritual

A fascinating way in which T.I.C.D. has attempted to link members of the urban middle classes to rural people is through a reconception of the traditional Phapa ritual. The Phapa (wilderness robes) ceremony is an offering of robes and other gifts to the monks for their daily needs. It is similar to another, better-known ritual, the traditional Kathin presentation. The Kathin however, is set at the end of the rainy season; the Phapa ceremony can take place at any time. Phapa generally is less formal and less costly. Kathin is more exclusively centered on the presentation of robes; Phapa may include smaller items for the monk's use--food, cigarettes, sweets, and money. One typical manner of presenting the gifts is to cut a small tree, decorate its branches with the gifts, and place it in the monastery before the assembled monks.

The T.I.C.D. has reinterpreted the Phapa ritual as an occasion for donating rice through village wats to establish rice banks or rice cooperatives. This project was initiated in Tha Mafaiwan village, Chaiyaphum province, in 1981. The Phapa ceremony became a pilgrimage to this small village for the giving of rice (or funds to buy rice) to the village wat. Tha Mafaiwan village is a poor village in the depressed northeast part of Thailand where 272 farming families live in a flat area that was formerly a forest reserve at the base of a small mountain range. Some wood is cut for sale; tapioca, maize, and rice are raised; there are a few government jobs in reforestation. Some cattle are raised and traded, and upland vegetables such as peppers and cabbages are grown. But rice can only be grown in some of the lowland that retains water.

About 80 percent of the village families are indebted to the extent of 10,000 baht per family--two or three times the per capita yearly income in the northeast. Indebtedness stems from high interest rates--up to 200 percent a year. Since not enough rice is grown in the village for local consumption, families are often forced to purchase rice, and thereby adding to their debts. T.I.C.D. and other cooperating groups have worked through the abbot of the Tha Mafaiwan wat to expand the capital of a beginning rice cooperative whose purposes are to be able to sell rice reasonably during shortages and to seek assistance from government sources for increasing year-round yields of rice.

Converting the Phapa ceremony into a grain ritual encourages people to donate rice to expand the cooperative. In 1981, during the Buddhist "Lenten" season, 1,200 kilos of rice and 72,789 baht were collected. Fifty-three people traveled from Bangkok and other places to make donations at the Phapa ceremony and stay in the village for a few days. Among the "pilgrims" were doctors and nurses who set up clinics. Students conducted some cultural events and put on entertainments for village children. They concentrated on getting to know the people in the village and working with the wat and the people to enable them to meet their own needs.

The organizers in their evaluation said they felt villagers had a sense of being part of a concerned community, which also helped overcome their sense of isolation. The villagers made plans to carry on with developing the cooperative. It was also noted that, although the Phapa ceremony is essentially Buddhist, Catholics, Protestants, and Muslims also participated.

The Phapa ceremony, like other rituals, is going through some reevaluation among Thais. Some observers have noted that in times past, giving to the monastery was chiefly an act of accumulating merit for the giver. But Jane Bunnag suggests that contributions to the wat may be increasingly evaluated by the purity of the giver's intention as well as the usefulness of the act or the gift itself. If this shift of meaning is actually taking place, T.I.C.D.'s reinterpretation of the Phapa ceremony is a creative social extension of that trend.[10]

T.I.C.D. Programs for Novices and Monks

Another focus of T.I.C.D.'s effort has been its work in seminars and training programs for samanera (novices) and bhikkhus (monks). These have been held in Bangkok, at Suan Mokh (the wat of Buddhadasa Bhikkhu), and in other rural areas. Their purpose has been to promote practical work in community analysis and development as well as discussion and interpretation of broader social issues. These seminars have struggled with the problem of traditional Buddhism in a contemporary society that seems to be moving on the path of competitive materialism, undermining the role of the monks in village settings. While there is a danger of romanticizing both the traditional village and the function of the monks, it is true that they often served as educators, agricultural advisers, and healers. To some extent the Sangha also provided a paradigm of detachment from material gain and a carefree existence that was exemplary in Thai society. How is the Sangha to deal with this perceived decline in its traditional role? It sees increasing urbanization, commercialization, and the spread of western culture and life styles as threats to the influence of the wat. In addition to the government's assumption of many educational responsibilities, other aspects of the bureaucracy, public and private, impinge on the monks' influence.

How does the example of simplicity, detachment, and earning of merit that was part of the Sangha paradigm bear on the acquisitive corporate and industrial society? T.I.C.D. in its seminars and training programs demonstrates its hope that the Buddhist tradition and its vision of life have religious resources to meet these challenges. T.I.C.D. started one training school for novices and monks in 1981 in Surathani province. Its objectives are to encourage social service, develop "the critical mind so that they [the monks] could understand the realities of this society . . . [and] learn to be analytical toward their communities . . . . Let them see that work is a practice of dharma itself . . .[including] practical skills such as health care, construction, agriculture and craftsmanship.[11] This program involves thirty trainees a year. After the first year of operation it was found that the objectives and curriculum of the school had application to some youth in the area who were not monks. Some young laymen, it seemed, were interested in becoming monks for the purpose of receiving the benefit of the training. Since it is common in Thailand for young monks to disrobe after a time to re-enter lay life, this does not pose any great difficulty. At any one time, there are about 100,000 novices in Thailand. Only about a third of the monks are considered permanent. Thus the Samanera Training School is viewed as having a broader influence than simply on the so-called permanent monks.

Study of Buddhadasa Bhikkhu's Teachings

It has been noted that T.I.C.D. has as one of its projects a year-long study of the well-known Thai Buddhist monk and intellectual, Buddhadasa Bhikkhu. T.I.C.D. is a small but creative association of youths and adults working at the grass roots for social reconstruction and economic justice. Buddhadasa, on the other hand, is very well known nationally, and his influence has been felt in many quarters. He has succinct, albeit general, teachings on social problems and the nation's contemporary trauma, but his chief mission is religious reconception and renewal of the fundamentals of Buddhism as he understands them. Buddhadasa's reforming view of Buddhism provides the religious basis of T.I.C.D.'s understanding and action. His many-faceted thought may be seen in at least three dimensions: (1) his interpretation of Buddhism and meditation, (2) his view of Christianity and its relation to Buddhism, and (3) his social criticism. We are fortunate that some of his writings are available in English.[12] We also have a succinct treatment of his thought by Donald K. Swearer.[13]

Buddhadasa's religious teaching emphasizes the reality of the truth and the reality of enlightenment, both as realized in the here-and-now and as inspiring a vision of the future. As he sees it, religious transformation is built on the capacity of the self to reach beyond self-delusion, greed, and hate and to change itself to accord with a greater sense of reality, freedom, and compassion. He articulates this process with a full epistemological treatment of the steps in the Buddhist approach to knowledge. For example, he says that we must analyze the body, the mind, and the emotions to raise our awareness of our relations with persons and with nature. Understanding how we relate to them enables us to be more self-conscious about unwise attachments and freer to perceive reality. Buddhadasa freely uses insights from Mahayana Buddhism and the teaching of _Sunyata_ to mean that our minds should be free and unbound. He uses the common Thai expression _jit waang_, "free time" or "unoccupied," to express the force of _Sunyata_.

To the extent we can penetrate through ignorant cravings or attachments that are the result of illusions, we are in the "void". Hence in speaking of persons, _detachment_ or _disiniterest_ or _freedom_ may be a better word than _void_ or _emptiness_. What is intended . . . true being. Thus _Sunyata_ is the state in which the mind, indeed the whole being, is unobstructed by false realities and therefore free to make choices. As Swearer interprets this teaching, the "move from samsara to nirvana is not a journey to a 'separate reality', but a way from attachment to non-attachment, from greed and anxiety to calm and equanimity, or from 'self' to 'not self'."[14] Buddhadasa writes, "The void in the common language of ignorant people means nothing exists, but in the language of the Buddha, the Enlightened 'One', the word 'void' means everything exists, but there is no attachment to any of it in terms of 'I' or 'mine'. . . ."[15] Buddhadasa likes to repeat these lines of admonition:

> Do work of all kinds with a mind that is void.
> And then to the voidness give all the fruits.
> Take food of the voidness as to the Holy Saints.
> And lo! You are dead to yourself from the very
> beginning.

The free self does not cling compulsively or crave ignorantly but controls its mind. Its freedom comes with the kind of control that meditation produces. Buddhadasa speaks of meditation as a stake used to tether the mind, like a stake used by a trainer to tie a wild monkey in order to tame him into gentleness.

He also uses the analogy of sharpening a knife for better cutting, or polishing a mirror to see more clearly. Meditation is the discipline to use for gaining sharper, clearer self-direction.

Buddhadasa emphasizes the Theravada meditation of "breathing mindfulness" to calm or center the mind--to achieve a sense of sustained control that enables us to attain an inner cohesiveness in which we relate to ourselves and to our surroundings with equanimity. With the mind both calm and alert, we are free from trivial or impulsive distractions and acquire a truer view of reality.

Breathing meditation starts with simple exercises in exhaling and inhaling as a conscious process, counting breathing rhythms of the moving abdominal wall or the "gateway" of breath, the nostrils. In Buddhism this meditation is best done with an experienced teacher who can modify instruction according to the needs and temperament of the person. Buddhadasa stresses, however, that this discipline is available to the ordinary person and that control is not a supernatural feat exclusive to saints. Although Buddhadasa recognizes various highly disciplined and unusual states of mind (_jhanas_) described in Buddhist teachings, he maintains that the fruits of insight meditation are available to all and that the meditative state of mind does not take one out of functioning in society but empowers one to engage in practical activity. The fruits of meditation are coolness or calmness of mind, which enables one to relate to others in compassion.

A second focus of Buddhadasa's thought is the relationship between Christianity and Buddhism. His Sinclair Thompson Memorial Lectures, given at the Thailand Theological Seminary in 1967, entitled _Christianity and Buddhism_, are his most systematic treatment of this topic; there are also scattered references to Christianity in his other writings.[16] His interpretations raise issues for both Buddhists and Christians, and neither group may be entirely happy with his winnowing out the "chaff" of religion. For example, he wants to cut through the rhetoric of doctrinal debates. "In our comparative study of religion we should compare religion straight-forwardly without being considerate of anybody."[17] He believes that modern scholars "have their heads so full of different scriptural facts that they find themselves lost in the jungle of the scriptures."[18] In his opinion, only a fourth of the Bible contains the actual teachings of Jesus--and that is quite enough for emancipation. He is willing to let "the lengthy Old Testament" go.[19] "Even the short message as contained in the few pages of the Sermon on the Mount in the book of Matthew is far more than enough and complete for practice to attain emancipation."[20] He passes a similar judgment on Buddhism. Buddhist monks often teach simply the outward form of Buddhism without grasping the sense of Dharma, whose essence is to eschew attachment to anything whatsoever, to stop thinking "I" and "mine". One difference he sees between Christianity and Buddhism is that the former involves external help (grace) and the latter prefers the way of "internal" help, depending on natural resources in human existence.[21]

Beyond this single difference he attempts to distinguish among kinds of religion by their chief characteristics: (1) magic, (2) religion based on faith and prayer, (3) religion based on the self-help principle of karma, (4) the religion of wisdom and reason, (5) the religion of peace based on non-violence, and finally (6) the religion of loving and giving for others. There is no religion marked by only one characteristic. Central to his attempt at what might be called a reconciling reinterpretation is his suggestion that "all religions in the world have something in common which is the backbone and essence in terms of Karma . . . . By karma or action . . . is meant the practice which brings man into relationship with God."[22] He suggests that God may be conceived as a person, as a power, or as a condition. The only characteristic required of "God" is the overcoming of suffering. In so far as Jesus assists us in achieving a reality that overcomes suffering, Jesus is the son of God--one of the victors over suffering who are recognized as important in Buddhism. Since Christianity, like Buddhism, is a religion of wisdom and karma, Buddhadasa ingeniously concludes that we can be both Christian and Buddhist at the same time.[23]

In his thought, the spirit of God can best be interpreted as that which takes away the suffering of man through insight into the nature of reality. God is thus interpreted as Dharma. Those who have truly absorbed themselves into God or Dharma equally find meaning in life.[24] Redemption may be interpreted in the Buddhist sense as "the development of Perfections in order to remove mankind from all sufferings."[25] In this sense the Dharma is the "World Saviour" or redeemer. However, Dharma is not a personal God.[26] As an impersonal God, Dharma already exists as a refuge. One cannot escape the impression that Buddhatat's most comprehensive and all-embracing term is Dharma:

> Now let us turn our attention to the fact that non-attachment, which is the highest Dharma or Truth, is something wonderful, valuable, and extraordinary. It is the heart of every religion. It is the essence of Dharma. If there is a God, he is found here.[27]

This sense of reality that we achieve through nonattachment enables us to have a sense of relatedness to all life; this is the religious foundation of Buddhadasa's social thought. The problem we all share is the difficulty of suffering (dukkha). The beginning of compassion and social thought is the sense that as finite beings we struggle together to realize our true natures. Dukkha in its various dimensions is realized as a social and personal experience. We are all related in our common problems of craving and clinging and in our need to cool the fever of greed, hatred, and delusion, which are the causes of our ignorant craving. Once we grasp that we are all interdependent, that we are part of the constantly changing inflow of existence, we have the basis of acting with nonattachment. Buddhadasa applies his sense of the here-and-now to the practice of metta and karma. His is a thoughtful historical perspective, but he is more concerned with the actual practice of metta. "One begins with the practice."[28]

Buddhadasa applies his sense of practice in the present to several social-economic issues. He criticizes competitive materialism, for it may "suck up the benefit of others for the sake of men who belong to the system by hidden, roundabout and clever ways."[29] He applies his criticism to countries on both sides of the Iron Curtain. He suggests we must seriously ask such questions as

> How does self-centeredness, both in the form of capitalism and proletarianism, arise in the world? How can we come to love others in the same way as we love ourselves? How can the capitalist regard the proletarian as his son? . . . Why does the capitalist not believe in God who requires him to seek and possess as much as necessary (for his own livelihood) and use what is left over to support others, as parents would support their children?[30]

Buddhadasa's penetrating ethical skepticism enables him to suggest that adherents of dialectical materialism who talk about the law of nature or the law of science may be actually referring to the same phenomenon as those who talk about God. Perhaps they are, if both are seriously concerned for solving "the problems of birth, aging, and death," or human suffering.

Perhaps Buddhadasa may be faulted for too quickly seeking the similarities to Dharma in quite diverse ways of thinking. On the other hand, he raises important issues for the understanding of the Dharma, and he demonstrates its pertinence to immediate social conflict. He further suggests that the Dharma must come into play in the world while the fighting is going on between the communist and capitalist worlds: we cannot wishfully wait for some idyllic moment without conflict. His argument is directed as much to Buddhists as to non-Buddhists. In addressing the World Fellowship of Buddhists in 1970, he answered the question, Should Buddhists play a leadership role in the affairs of the world? by stressing the teaching of the Buddha: "The Tathagata [or Buddha] is born in the world for the happiness of all beings, including gods and men. The Dharma and Vinaya of the Tathagatha is present in the world for the happiness of all beings including gods and men." And he repeats the injunction of the Buddha in sending out the first group of monks: "Go you forth, Oh Bhikkhus . . . to preach the divine life for the benefit and happiness of the world."[31]

Although he conceives socialism to be less acquisitive and competitive than capitalism, he thinks it too may breed conflict and serve materialism.[32] Socialism in his sense is based on sangama-niyama, or the way of restraint in the interest of others. As Donald Swearer comments, Bhuddhadasa has "created a 'socialistic' monastic community (sangama-niyama) where all labor for the good of the whole and for the truth."[33] Such problems as population growth, he believes, should be considered in the light of available resources, economic growth, production, and equitable distribution. When asked for actual instances of the practice of sangama-niyama, Bhuddhadasa suggests that in ancient Thailand it was the way that rulers dealt with the ruled: even slaves (corvee labor) were considered to be part of the sharing community. But as he looks to the future, he talks about his hope that the United Nations or some international organization may play a creative role in international justice and peace.

The Rice Phapa Ceremony is a traditional rite of giving gifts to the Buddhist Wat (Temple). The Thai Interreligious Commission on Development demonstrates in the following report a creative reconception of traditional religious practices in order to provide a positive response to economic need.

A Buddhist monk is described as appealing to merit making as a way to establish a rice bank. This is more effective than simply preaching the five precepts. Merit making is conceived of as a means to a broader and wholistic social relationship rather than merely giving alms to the monk or the temple.

A TICD RICE BANK SEMINAR

There are many different approaches to community development. But usually the model is imported from outside. There has been too little respect for local initiatives, and there has been too little praise for traditional values. Working with monks, we feel that we can learn much from them. They try to bridge the gap between traditional values and modern concepts of progress. They can do so with skill and wisdom. In this seminar, theory came together with practice, and rational thoughts were brought up in the light of traditional values. The rice bank is one of the cooperative savings methods. It is a way to strengthen village economies. Though it does not change the exploitative network, it helps to establish a stronghold of local bargaining power, and it is also a means to educate people toward a more cooperative strategy. There are many monks involved in rice-bank projects. The difference between secular rice banks and rice banks organized by monks can be seen clearly. In both cases the idea comes from outside, but secular rice banks are implemented without enough understanding of village life, while the ones organized by monks incorporate the cultural heritage. From the monks, we have many kinds of rice banks with different rules and regulations--even with different approaches. The following will be about two examples of these different kinds of initiatives and opinions on rice banks described at our recent seminar. The monks speak of their own experiences.

Rice Bank and Dhamma

Pra Athikarn Sanon Thavaro is the abbot of Kasanuan Temple, Rakornrajasima Province.

> I held that genuine trust from the people must come first. I had been working at that place for six years, starting by preaching the five precepts in order to prevent villagers from falling into degraded paths. There were some who could follow, but many failed. Hence I

thought that there should be other means or vehicles to lead the people towards the right direction. For the people would always proclaim, "We cannot eat Dhamma instead of rice; if we observe the precepts, we will be starving. Only the rich can observe the precepts."

So the ideas of Pra Banjat came to mind. I thought that I should adapt the traditional way of merit-making so that it would be more practical. People used to believe that merit-making was to do or to give things useful for the temple. That was the old belief. I tried to give a new understanding of it. I told the people that merit-making could be done to any other person, monks or not, and it could be done anywhere: there was no need that it must only be performed within the temple compound.

Then I thought that the villagers had been spending a lot of money on merit-making, especially on the special religious days which took place throughout the year. And as I could not stop them, I would rather change my role. So I became a cooperative staff member, collecting their money for them. According to the Lord Buddha's teaching, monks should not consume more things than necessary, and what was left should be returned to the people. So when we received more than we really needed, we would spend the rest buying rice and putting it in a storehouse for the people. Sometimes we decided to buy buffaloes to form a buffalo bank. The villagers agreed with this idea from the very beginning. And sometimes there were people from other places (usually middle-class people from towns) coming to offer robes for monks after the rainy season. Together with the robes, they also offered other things, as well as money. Usually, this money would be used for the maintenance of the temple. But I asked these people if I could use this money to help the poor. They agreed with

> me on my idea. They were glad that their offerings would be useful to the poor people. I felt that these sacrifices and solidarity would bring us nearer to the Dhamma.

And here is a contribution from another monk: Pra Khumkhien Suwanno, the abbot of Tha Maphaiwan Temple, Chayapoom Province:

> Our main pursuit is the Dhamma. We would like to solve the problems of villagers spiritually as well as economically. And in my village, the concrete problem is the lack of rice. The villagers were not united in trying to solve their own problems. The rice cooperative here in Tha Maphaiwan is not a success. I think that I have committed a mistake. For it was pushed forth mostly by me instead of being initiated by the people.
>
> From the beginning, I did not conceive of the direction that I would have taken later on. I started with preaching. This village was a new village; people had come from many places. There were also many outlaws who wanted to start new lives but were still violent. They liked gambling and led their lives in degraded ways. I thought that there should be monks working in this kind of village, so I went there. In fact, the people there had to face a lot of difficulties: they were starving. When I saw the problems more clearly, I tried to find some means to solve the problems. I discussed it with the people. I asked them whether they were really poor, and if they were really poor, whether they could find some ways to help each other. Trusting me as a monk, they tried to find some ways to solve the problems with me.
>
> From these experiences, I think that economic well-being should not be an end. It may come as a result of cooperative activities, but we should not pursue it as it if were the only objective. The priority is how we can

lead people to love each other and help each other. Loving each other, they will be more readily responsive to the wisdom of the Dhamma; without love, it will not be possible.

The Rice Phapa, a Tradition

Performing the Phapa ceremony has been a Buddhist tradition since olden times. It stemmed from the laymen's desire to provide monks and novices with daily requisites so that they could spend their lives in a manner becoming their status and perform their religious duties smoothly. This would not only prolong the religious faith but also benefit the surrounding communities, since in olden times the temple was both the spiritual and social center of the community. For example, it was the school, the hospital, the club, and the entertainment place. All the things that the local people gave the temple on various occasions, including these given during the Phapa Ceremony, would eventually benefit the local people.

Rice Phapa for the Sake of the Temple and the Local People

At present, although the Phapa ceremony is still a popular tradition among the Buddhists, its purpose has deviated from promoting the monks' livelihood for the welfare of the whole community to erecting permanent structures for the dominance and grace of the temple. The latter purpose is not conducive to prolonging the religious faith, nor is it really beneficial to the community. The Phapa Ceremony as it is usually performed now tends to cause substantial loss of resources. It is therefore imperative that the tradition be modified to bring it up to date by promoting the role of the monk as the leader in helping the community in conjunction with his role as the community's spiritual leader.

One form of the Phapa ceremony that will benefit the community is the Rice Phapa, which will relieve great numbers of people in rural areas who have to go into debt to buy rice at high prices for consumption before the harvest season. A good example is the villagers at Tha Mafaiwan Village, a big village of 272 families (1,600 persons) situated on the Laenda Mount, a mountain range in Kaengkhro District, Chaiyaphum Province. It is inaccessible to cars during the rainy season. The only way to reach it is to walk uphill for an hour through Kaengkhro District. The villagers' original occupation was growing rice in dry fields, but the yield was rather poor. They therefore switched to growing tapioca and maize during the past few years. As a result, they have the problem of finding rice for consumption because they must go uphill and downhill to buy rice. During the rainy season traveling is especially difficult. If they buy rice at the village, they have to pay a lot more (700 baht per sack on credit), running deeper into debt.

Early this year Phra Khamkhian Suwanno, the abbot of the Tha Mafaiwan Temple, initiated a project for selling cheap rice to the villagers. At present the villagers have a plan to expand the capital and register a rice cooperative, with the help of government authorities, so as to be able to produce sufficient amounts of rice to members all year round. However, the capital obtained through the cooperation between the temple and the villagers is insufficient to establish a cooperative that can meet the villagers' needs. Therefore, additional capital is needed.

Part of the money to help boost the rice cooperative will come from performing the Phapa ceremony (also known as the Rice Phapa ceremony). But instead of giving donations to the temple for erecting permanent structures, this time benevolent individuals will donate rice or money to the Tha Mafaiwan Temple so that the temple will have more capital to operate the cooperative and be able to lend rice to the villagers for consumption when rice is scarce. The villagers will pay back the rice to the cooperative later.

To make merit in this manner is in accordance with the principles of Buddhism: it not only makes the temple the breeding ground for good deeds that the villagers can depend on, both materially and spiritually; it also shows a benevolent attitude towards fellow countrymen who are poorer and who suffer more hardships. Helping other people overcome their hardships in accordance with our capabilities, our benevolent minds, and our desire to help our fellow countrymen is regarded as the key to the principles and teachings of Buddhism.

Rice Bank: Is There a Best Way to Organize?

The formal organization of a rice bank begins with members, rules, and regulations. Under this arrangement, only members can borrow rice. But Chao Atthikan Roonmee, the abbot of Takolai Temple in Burirum Province, told us, "When the poor are starving, you should not care much about regulations. Give them rice without any conditions. It is a way to build up good will. People will then donate more rice. And when you have enough rice, then you can have rules and regulations."

At the village of Ara Khumkhien, villagers make their livelihood by growing cassava, corn, and other crops; they do not grow rice. Before any initiatives were taken, they had to buy very expensive rice. After discussing ways to buy cheaper rice, they set up a rice cooperative. Then they could buy cheaper rice, and the profits from the cooperative would also be theirs.

Pragruphiphitprachanath, the abbot of Samaggi Temple, Surin Province, did not agree wholeheartedly that rice donated for the temple should all go to the rice bank. He said that we should divide rice into three portions: one for the rice bank, one for the immediate welfare of those who were starving, and one for the temple. So there are many ways to organize a rice bank. There is no readymade answer for all; it depends on the background of each particular village.

(TICD *Newsletter* No. I, January-April 1983)

VI

ASIAN CULTURAL FORUM ON DEVELOPMENT

The Beginnings of ACFOD

In March, 1973, as a by-product of the Food and Agriculture Organization's "Action for Development" campaign, a group of concerned leaders from the major religious groups in Asia--Buddhist, Hindu, Muslim, and Christian--met together in Bangkok. In subsequent meetings that year, they formed an Asia-wide coalition on development and justice. Between 1973 and 1975, the words justice and religious appeared in the new organization's name. In June, 1975, the name Asian Cultural Forum on Development was formally adopted. The title was intended to symbolize the inclusiveness of participants--among them some who are not specifically religious. The ACFOD constitution contains a statement of principles recognizing that "the religions of Asia offer potential resources for working together in a common concern for the development of the peoples of Asia."[1]

ACFOD is a Bangkok-based network of groups aiming at "integral development," a concept that includes "the socio-economic and religio-cultural advancement of peoples." Its distinctive role is to link grass-roots organizations and leaders concerned with economic justice and development and to encourage sharing and interaction among them. Eight or nine countries were involved in the initial organization. Now as many as fourteen countries participate in the network, with ten of them having members on the coordinating team: Bangladesh, India, Indonesia, Japan, Malaysia, Nepal, New Zealand, Philippines, Sri Lanka, and Thailand. Visits have been initiated in an effort to establish links with Burma and China. ACFOD leaders have visited Vietnam, Laos, and Kampuchea in attempts to develop cross-national communication and understanding.

The first coordinator was Father Stanislaus Fernando of Sri Lanka. Some initial funding came from the World Council of Churches and the Papal

Commission on Peace and Justice. Christian participants apparently recognized their minority status in Asia and saw the wisdom of sharing leadership with those of other faiths. In 1979 Sulak Sivaraksa, a Buddhist layman and Thai social critic, was elected coordinator and Bamrung Boonpanya, a Thai, as associate coordinator. (Sulak had been a member of the coordinating team except during 1977 when he was forced to remain abroad because of political repression in Thailand. A bookstore that he and his wife operated was raided by forces of the military government during that year in what seemed to be a search for subversive materials.) Sulak worked extensively with students, Buddhist monks, village wats, the Siam Society, and interfaith groups. His books Siam in Crisis and A Buddhist Vision for Renewing Society are sharply articulate reflections on and criticisms of Thai society and Thai Buddhism. He holds that the error of western technocratic notions of development is that they measure development by quantity or aggregate growth and hold that "the more production the better, as long as there is just distribution."[2] The industrial model of development, he claims, has lost sight of the importance of awakening to self-knowledge and feeling a profound sense of solidarity with others and with nature. He sees both Marxism and capitalism as built on essentially western cognitive models and proposes instead the Buddhist middle path as a perspective on the quality of a human economy.

Sulak believes that development has "increasingly become the development of the rich countries and the anti-development of the poor countries, particularly the broad agrarian populations of the latter." Asian people need to "develop an awareness of their conditions and the strength to strive towards meaningful participation in . . . their own process of change."[3]

The range of ACFOD's education and action endeavors is simultaneously grass-roots, international, and pluralistic. ACFOD is not a religious organization as such, but from its inception it has included religious aims and religious leaders. It will be instructive, therefore, to deal first with the religious dimensions of its work.

ACFOD's Religious Activities

In the first of ACFOD's newsletters, published in January, 1976, it was recognized that the traditions, cultures, and languages of Asia were religious--Buddhist, Islamic, Hindu, or Christian. "But the social service that these major religions have hitherto played has been inadequate. Too often it has tended to be reactionary."[4] ACFOD's appeal called for a radical redefinition of roles and for regional initiatives "sustained by action programmes and well-documented research projects undertaken by people, organizations, and people-oriented individuals."[5]

In December of 1977, members of the ACFOD coordinating team met for their annual year-end meeting in Jakarta, Indonesia. Having held all its previous meetings in Bangkok, the team attempted to add field visits to its business sessions. A review of direction occurred at this meeting. A report on the deliberations acknowledged that

> Foremost among the vision of ACFOD is the role of religion. . . . Yet it is still a subject of tension, for there are two views of it: one that it supports the status quo and the other that concerns itself with the just relationship of man with his fellowman and a greater Being.[6]

In June, 1977, ACFOD held a joint workshop with FAO in Bangkok. Participating were forty-seven persons from sixteen countries and a broad spectrum of religions and cultures from both the East and the West. For this workshop a questionnaire had been sent to over sixty Asians to gather data on attitudes toward nongovernmental organizations having some role in rural development action.

One question asked about the potential of religious groups for creating a force for development. Responses to this question cited some peasant leaders in Indonesia, Muslim groups in the Philippines, socially oriented Buddhist monks in Sri Lanka, and Catholic priests in the Philippines as examples of helpful allies in the fight against socioeconomic injustice. Other respondents, although feeling that individual religious leaders might play important roles in the struggle for justice, indicated that religious organizations as such, because of their structure and recent history, were not able to effectively respond. Several other reasons were given for the inactivity or inability of religious groups in the work for development and justice: (1) Religious organizations, whether Buddhist, Christian, Hindu, or Islamic, appeared to be safeguarding their lands and other property and furthering their own narrow interests. (2) Christian organizations were still largely dependent on aid from overseas, and winning converts seemed to be their chief occupation. (3) Unconscious yet deeply imbedded feelings of superiority within each religion made it difficult for them to coordinate with each other. (4) A majority of the priests of all faiths were still very conservative, fearing that openness might lead to a loss of identity with the religious beliefs and values of their particular religion or order.[7]

At the same meeting the future selection of participants for ACFOD's Development Workers' Program was considered. Three implicit criteria were to determine the choice of nominees from each country: grass-roots involvement, organizational support, and adherence to the "predominant religion of the country" from which they came. In evaluations of The Development Workers' Program, one result mentioned was the enhanced awareness of the function of religion in the development process--for example, Buddhist monks working with the village people of Sri Lanka and priests participating in the conscientization work of the church in the Philippines. However, the consensus was that most of the religious institutions had become identified with social elites and were resistant to change.[8]

The coordinator of ACFOD reported at the same meeting that an ACFOD leader had been in touch with the World Fellowship of Buddhists regarding a proposal to hold a seminar on "The Role of Religion in Integrated Development with Special Emphasis on the Buddhist Traditions of Thailand and Sri Lanka." Unfortunately, nothing came of this intiative. The World Fellowship of Buddhists held its own conference on "Survival and Development" in June, 1982, in Colombo.

An early ACFOD newsletter commented on the contemporary response of Buddhism to economic development and justice:

> [There is] the dawning of a realization in sections of the Buddhist Sangha in Sri Lanka and Thailand that religion and religious personnel must return to fulfill the function of a people's dharma. The return, it is true, would imply a going back before moving forward and could thus be expected to arouse raised eyebrows on the part of western educated bourgeoisie and elite. Yet the significance of such development must not be minimized or overlooked."[9]

Sulak Sivaraksa, the ACFOD's coordinator, in the Thompson Memorial Lecture given in 1976 in Chiang Mai, Thailand, expressed this dynamic thus:

> It is not too late, especially in the rural areas where religion is still a powerful force, for religion to play a constructive role in development, but it must understand the situation in its totality. When there is no understanding, religion usually falls into one of two errors. It either goes along unthinkingly with the materialism of the secular development or else it blindly opposes the development. But if religious leaders understand both their own heritage and the dynamics of the new situation, then the masses will support them in constructive change toward purity of heart and justice."[10]

An outstanding intercountry dialogue was organized by ACFOD in the spring of 1981, when it brought a group of eight Sri Lankan religious leaders engaged in development activity to Thailand and in took a group of Thai leaders to Sri Lanka. In Thailand there were visits to cooperative farm projects, refugee camps, buffalo banks, health care projects in folk medicine, monks' training institutions, women's organizations, slum and welfare work, tribal areas, and organizations trying to raise the consciousness of social injustice. In both countries the group witnessed country festivals, lived in temples, and visited with marginal economic groups. Several groups with a program of radical political criticism were contacted. This program not only enlarged the participants' perspectives on what religious groups could do in a great variety of practical ways but also established interreligious contacts that they found very deepening.

At the seventeenth meeting of the ACFOD coordinating team in June of 1982 in Singapore, it was agreed that interreligious "dialogue-in-action" should be continued and promoted at both the national and regional levels.

ACFOD Development Efforts

The ACFOD action program has had several foci. It has emphasized Development Workers' Training Programs, started in 1976. The 1977 evaluation described the program as "an experience in dialogical training in participatory development."[11] Each year participants from six or seven countries (Bangladesh, India, Indonesia, Malaysia, Philippines, Sri Lanka, Thailand) have engaged in a three-month program of field visits of seven to ten days to each other's areas of work, sharing problems and experiences, living in villages, and receiving training in community analysis and development work. The workers represent Muslim, Hindu, Christian, and Buddhist backgrounds, the largest number being Buddhist. Out of the Development Workers' Training Program have come (1) a new sense of the value of communication with grass-roots development workers and (2) the view that each national group should experiment with its own program, supplemented by regional programs of a special character. For example, a workshop on low-cost audiovisual media was held in March, 1976, in Manila with seven countries represented and some NGO's. It focused on the use of common materials, such as biscuit tins, cardboard boxes, and magnifying lenses in constructing simple but effective projections. Samples of film strips and tapes produced and used by various village movements were shown and discussed.

In 1976 a successful workshop on Asian rural drama was held in the Philippines. At present ACFOD has plans for working with a Philippine group to establish contacts and exchanges among drama groups.

Another regional training program was a workshop for fishermen in Kottayam, Kerala, in September of 1980 that brought together small-scale fishermen from Sri Lanka, Bangladesh, Tamilnadu, Kerala, and Malaysia. Follow-up activities have included Fishnet, a newsletter in different languages. An interesting focus at these fishermen's training programs has been "macro-analysis and micro-involvement," as it was expressed by one leader.[12]

Several difficulties confront small fishermen: (1) They once represented the citadel of indigenous technology, but now major international companies are using large mechanized trawlers, thus depriving them of their livelihood. (2) The use of mechanized trawlers has also led to over-fishing, disturbance to spawning areas, and depletion of some species of fish. (3) Increased industrialization near some seaports and large-scale use of agricultural fertilizers have produced effluents that have polluted inland and coastal fishing areas. (4) The Coast Guard is inadequate to enforce fishing regulations. (5) In order to promote tourism, many Asian governments subsidize hotel and resort development, thereby squeezing out fishing villages by making housing expensive.

ACFOD is primarily a regional network, but since its coordinator and associate coordinator are Thai and its headquarters are in Bangkok, much of its work and influence are concentrated in Thailand. There is a network of village level organizations, individual workers, Buddhist wats, and student groups with relationships to ACFOD. Coordinator Sulak has worked closely with monks at Wat Tongonappakun in Bangkok and Wat Yokrabat, about an hour's drive south of Bangkok. He maintains a helpful relationship with Buddhatat Bhikkhu at Wat Suan Mok. (Buddhatat is a reforming intellectual figure in the Sangha who emphasizes that nirvana is an experience here and now rather that in some nebulous future. His writings on politics, including his discussion of Buddhist socialism, have had an impact on many. Buddhatat's work was described at greater length in chapter 5.)

Praku Sakorn, the abbot of Wat Yokrabat, achieved a measure of unity and social consciousness in his impoverished community by organizing people to build dikes and canals to help desalinate the soil. Landowners donated some of their property to make the canal possible. Monks worked together with laymen on the project. The irrigation canal, winding like a ribbon through the parched countryside, stands as a vivid reminder of community action and cooperation.

Praku Sakorn also organized the planting of coconut as a secondary crop; in order to avoid middlemen, the people made their own sugar from coconuts, using traditional techniques. Credit unions, vegetable growing, irrigation projects are all being very systematically organized. Bhikkhus from other temples have come to visit and learn. Now a concerted effort is being made to improve the local high schools so as to encourage more young people to stay in the village. The recent decline in the world price of sugar has unfortunately held back the economic progress of the village.

ACFOD visitors to the village have recognized the dependence of the laity on the abbot--a strong and capable leader and effective organizer who has restored the centrality of the temple. Now the need for the development of lay leaders among the villagers is apparent.

ACFOD's associate coordinator, Bamrung Boonpanya , maintains contact with village workers from many groups. He spends much of his time visiting Thai villages and arranging contacts. He views ACFOD's work as keeping the intellectuals in touch with the villagers and raising the consciousness of the villagers. ACFOD in his words is "culture in action." His phrase indicates the need to be aware of all dimensions of the village culture--the interrelationships among land-holding patterns, tenancy, food needs and production, marketing problems, village leadership, health problems, and the religious situation. ACFOD's work is increasing the villagers' awareness of their own culture and their resources for participation and change in poverty and dependency. ACFOD's leaders know of the economic pressures that make many of the landless poor get poorer. Bamrung cites that fact that nearly 800,000 farmers move to the urban areas each year, mainly because they cannot earn an adequate income from the lands they have been working.

ACFOD has included Marxists as participants and members. It has, in fact, been able to maintain international ties among Christian Marxists, Buddhist Marxists, and secular Marxists, even though Marxism is largely underground and taboo in Thailand. Recent visits of ACFOD leaders to Burma, Vietnam, China, and Kampuchea have sought to establish communication with religious leaders and groups in those countries. Sulak is uneasy about dividing the world into "free world" and "communist" camps. He is a strong advocate of nonviolence and democratic social change but does not want to stereotype communism as a monolithic adversary.

The development priorities of ACFOD for the future are to identify and work with more peasant organizations, to find women's groups interested in raising the status of women, to publish more materials in Asian languages, and to strengthen the national organization's efforts for integral development.

Some of the Development Workers' projects have increased awareness of the barriers to justice that women face in some traditional village cultures. A partial summary of a workshop discussion among forty-two women from landless groups in Bangladesh depicts their downtrodden state:

> We have no specified hours of work. We work from before sunrise until the whole household falls asleep. We are forced to work in rich people's homes--husking, boiling, drying paddy, cooking, washing and performing other household chores. . . . Unlike the men, we have no definite wages and are dependent on the individual whim of our employers.
>
> If there is no child, the wife always gets the blame. When there are children, the burden of caring for them is solely the wife's concern.
>
> Education is not considered important for girls. Women are not allowed to express their opinions--even regarding their own marriage, or choosing an occupation.[13]

<u>Asian Action</u> has carried reports of women's issues from Malaysia, Bangladesh, India, Thailand, and Nepal. Early its editors discovered and published a vivid poem from Loyra Village, India:

I rise before dawn
While no one hears
Grinding maize-grain, singing
(Which no one hears)
And milk the buffalo
Warm under the thatch,

Send my child to scare the parrots
Send my husband to the field
Take his roti (bread) to the furrows
Wash the vessels at the cistern
Carry the water to the household
Churn the lassi (buttermilk) in the evening
Launder clothing in the noon-heat
Gather gobar in the morning
Suffer docile to my husband

Once a year a wedding feasts me
Once a year the Gavri dances
Once a year extend our family
Thrice a lifetime lose my baby
Once a week cry to my goddess
Into the thin morning air.[14]

Most of ACFOD's work to date has been with farmers, fishermen, and other rural people. Now it is planning a major program specifically for women. Sulak Sivaraksa noted at the September, 1981, council meeting held in Sri Lanka that, while there was growing participation of young people and grass-roots workers and groups, ACFOD programs drew very few women in. In November of 1983 ACFOD sponsored a Women's Workshop at Cha-Am, Thailand, with participants from Asian and Pacific countries. A three-year regional program was formulated dealing with population control, militarism, prostitution, violence against women, and conditions of women workers.

ACFOD programs have not until recently directly involved urban industrial workers, although its newsletter discusses many urban issues: slum eviction, tourism, pollution, child labor, human rights, and factory conditions. At the ACFOD council meeting in November of 1983, it was decided that there must be "supportive action to enhance the solidarity of workers in struggle in a particular country." ACFOD will initiate protests and boycotts in member countries and seek financial support for workers' causes. A newsletter with information on workers' conditions and their struggles will be published wherever possible in member countries, and an exchange program of activists to link workers' groups in several countries will be planned. An "Asian Workers Solidarity Links" organization and network was established to represent workers within the ACFOD structure and to carry out the new ACFOD program. Coordinator Sulak is already working with city wats and monks, social workers, human rights groups, and student activist groups centered in Bangkok. ACFOD has maintained a relationship with The Building Together Association, a group that promotes a practical, self-help approach to the housing problems of slum residents and other poor in Bangkok. The people of Jerusalem Village, an all-Muslim settlement in a slum area, were organized initially to reduce fire hazards by constructing their own fire protection system. The Building Together Association in Jerusalem village also concerns itself with the injustices in many slum evictions; in the process, it has transformed a low-income community into a self-help cooperative whose participants do most of the actual construction of homes. This community now has over eighty families participating.

The problems of tourism--which has boomed in Southeast Asia in the last decade--and the influence of American, German, and Japanese multinational corporations have also been subjects of repeated concern both at ACFOD meetings and in its publications. Special issues of Asian Action have centered on the nuclear armament issue in Japan, the Marshall Islands and New Zealand.

ACFOD's Dilemmas

One of the reasons ACFOD was initiated was the dissatisfaction Asian religious leaders felt in having to go to other western countries for conferences and activities on development. An Asian organization to coordinate Asian efforts for justice and development was the outcome.

But the very nature of ACFOD poses a dilemma: as a regional organization that provides a communication network among grass-roots groups, how much of its time and effort should be expended on a central secretariat and how much in development work at the grass-roots village level? Often at ACFOD's meetings there have been attempts to decentralize. For example, each country has been urged to organize its own activities and to prepare an issue of Asian Action. Another attempt has been to delegate to each national group the responsibility for developing a particular program emphasis--for example, workshops on drama to the Philippines. Another frustration of cross-international communication is illustrated in the fishermen's workshop and the Development Workers' Program. When people from seven Southeast Asian nations communicate, they must use English. Sinhalese is not spoken in Thailand nor Thai in Sri Lanka. Malayalam-speaking fishermen from Kerala may have to use English interpreters to talk with their Malay counterparts. Publishing Fishnet, a newsletter of the fishermen's development activities, has required considerable translation.

Another problem built into the ACFOD concept and practice is having intellectuals, both religious and secular, relating effectively to village people, often across national lines. The coordinating committee is composed of persons of international vision and experience who also network with many related organizations both in the region and throughout the world. The tension between time spent at the grass-roots and time spent on travel and interpretation to support groups is not easy to resolve.

Buddhist participation in ACFOD has been a distinct advantage. Until after the second World War, there was no international Buddhist organization, no established process for international discussion or criticism of social, economic, or political issues of common concern. Local and national Buddhist groups had no outlet for their concerns about such large issues as peace, development, or human rights. But the founding of the World Fellowship of Buddhists in the 1950s has made international conferences possible. Funding for the World Fellowship of Buddhists has been largely dependent on sympathetic governments. There has been a beginning of social criticism, such as the 1982 conference on "Survival and Development" held in Colombo, Sri Lanka. However, the Fellowship has taken almost no controversial stands or action on any social issue.

ACFOD may provide something of a model for regional collaboration on behalf of deprived people. It provides links among those outside governmental and official organizations who are concerned with social justice. By sparking the energies and yoking the efforts of like-minded people of differing religious and cultural traditions, it could provide the vision and community essential to a renewing of societies.

Two documents are provided as examples of the socio-economic criticisms of the Asian Forum on Cultural Development. The first, "Vision for the Eighties" gives an alternative perspective to the existing Asian social order. This statement has some similarities in form and content to that of Sarvodaya Shramadana in Chapter III. The ACFOD position includes specific criticism of the military and of the suppression of minorities and women. These aspects of the social order are not specifically mentioned in the earlier Sarvodaya statement.

The second example is a short version of a presentation to an FAO meeting by ACFOD coordinator Sulak Sivaraksa. His criticisms of existing attempts at land reform and the unequal distribution of income in Southeast Asian nations are particularly sharp. In the concluding chapter Sulak Sivaraksa's arrest and imprisonment by the Thai government is chronicled. His views of needed social and economic change and his criticism of the present power structure in Southeast Asia has led to the occasional suppression of his views by the Thai government.

VISION FOR THE EIGHTIES

ACFOD

AND THE NEW ASIA

The Fourth ACFOD Council meeting in November of 1983 reflected upon and analyzed the development experiences of Asian countries over the past two or three decades. The group identified the salient features that characterize these experiences and attempted a formulation of an alternative vision.

DOMINANT EXISTING SYSTEM	ACFOD VISION: TOWARDS AN ALTERNATE SYSTEM
1. Emphasis on economic growth and material needs.	1. Human-centered development of man and his potential (releases the creativity of people).
2. Serves dominant interests (land-lords, industrialists, local and foreign vested interests, bureau-cracy, and the military).	2. Serves people's interests (in particular the poor, the oppressed, and the disadvantaged).
3. Increasing dependence on foreign capital, aid, technology, and power.	3. National self-reliance.
4. Export-oriented production.	4. Production for use/to meet basic needs.
5. Inequality/control over re-sources by a few.	5. People's control over resources/ equal access to resources.
6. Depoliticization/domestication/ conditioning of people to pre-serve the status quo.	6. Awareness build-up/conscientization /politicization of the people for social change.
7. Fragmentation of people.	7. Organization of people and forging linkages/coalitions/unity among people's groups.

8. Urban bias.	8. Elimination of the contradiction between urban and rural.
9. Neglect/discrimination/oppression of women.	9. Integration of women.
10. Dominant culture.	10. People's culture and traditions.
11. Authoritarianism/centralization/ militarization.	11. Participatory democracy/decentral- ization/demilitarization.
12. Pollution and destruction of the environment/wasteful re- source use.	12. Harmony with the environment/con- servation of resources.
13. Suppression of minority rights and culture.	13. Respect for minority rights and cultures.
14. Power (domination)	14. Counter-power (liberation)

(Adapted from Asian Action, Newsletter of the Asian Cultural Forum on Development, January-February, 1984.)

Rural Poverty and Peasant Development in Southeast Asia

Sulak Sivaraksa
Coordinator, Asian Cultural Forum on Development

(A shortened version of a paper prepared by Sulak Sivaraksa in collaboration with Bamrung Bunpanaya and Jon Ungphakorn for the second International FFHC/AD Consultation, FAO, Rome, September, 1983)

1. Rural poverty in Southeast Asia

The lands of Southeast Asia, fertile and rich in natural resources, could undoubtedly provide sufficient food and a simple, pleasant life for their inhabitants. Why are 60 percent of the children in rural Thailand suffering from malnutrition? Why are the small fishermen on the coast of the Malaysian peninsula finding it difficult to survive? Why have millions of Indonesian peasants migrated to the slums of Jakarta? And why have so many Filipinos left their farms to be migrant workers in the Middle East and elsewhere?

There is an old Thai saying: "In the fields there is rice; in the water there are fish". This saying does not simply describe the abundance of food resources available to the populations of the region in the past; it also aptly describes the simple life of self-sufficiency that existed among village communities of Southeast Asia before the advent of colonialism and neocolonialism. In those days the communities farmed their own land and wove their own cloth. They were governed and protected by their own institutions: the family, the community, and the seniority system. Production was carried out by means of cooperation rather than competition and was geared to self-consumption, thus maintaining the unity and balance of nature.

I do not wish to imply that this was an idyllic life, free from suffering and exploitation. Of course there were disease, natural disasters, warfare, cultural repression of women, and so on. Also, village communities were not living in complete isolation. With the establishment of state power structures, land rights came under the control of the kings or state rulers. Village communities were required to pay taxes, dig canals, or even fight wars. Nevertheless, the relationship between the state and the peasantry was of a special nature in that the state dealt with village communities as a whole rather than with individuals or families. This allowed village communities to largely maintain their own independence in maintaining their production and in dealing with their own problems.

Colonialization and semicolonialization by the western powers brought about a basic upheaval in the village community production system. Buying and selling of commodities was introduced at the village level, resulting in the decline of traditional village handicrafts and a change from agricultural production for self-consumption to agricultural production for national and world markets. The self-sufficiency of village communities was gradually destroyed, while market forces over which the communities had no control dictated economic and social changes in the lives of the peasants. The establishment of agricultural export markets brought larger proportions of agricultural land under the direct ownership of the local aristocracies, thus increasing the number of sharecropping tenants. At the same time, foreign companies took over large tracts of land to establish rubber, sugarcane, coconut, and banana plantations, thus creating a new class of peasants, the agricultural laborers.

During the past fifty years, colonialism has been replaced by neocolonialism and "modernization." National governments who took over from colonial governments have continued and accelerated the penetration of market forces and capitalist systems of production throughout the rural areas of Southeast Asia. Rural development policies have concentrated on extending and strengthening infrastructures and on promoting investment in agriculture-related industries. Modernization has forced the peasants to depend on the market for clothing, electricity, water, fuel, construction materials, fertilizers, pesticides, livestock, and agricultural tools.

Undoubtedly, "rural development" and "modernization" as carried out by most Southeast Asian countries have brought about more efficient agricultural production and an increase in the average income and standard of living of the rural population. But the costs have been extremely high. Most of the benefits have fallen into the hands of the wealthy few, members of the upper and middle classes, such as the exporters, traders, landlords, plantation owners, agribusinesses, rice- and teak-mill owners, farmers with large landholdings, and businessmen, professionals, and high-ranking government officials in general. Economic growth has brought about a comparative growth of the upper and middle classes. Rural development has developed new power structures at the local level in rural areas. The growth of the elite has led to an ever-increasing demand for consumer goods from Japan and the West. This, in turn, requires increased agricultural exports and increased exploitation of the agricultural producers themselves.

Modernized agriculture has brought about large-scale depletion of natural resources. Forests are rapidly disappearing and, with them, much of the wildlife. The mudfishes and edible frogs that thrived in the rice fields and served as a rich source of food for the peasants are being killed by the use of chemical fertilizers and insecticides. Large-scale trawler fishing is depleting fish stocks and destroying the livelihoods of the small fishermen. It should be noted that the huge appropriation of natural resources and the resulting upheaval of the balance of nature has been mostly for the benefit of the "advanced" societies in Japan and the West and for the privileged elites in Southeast Asia, not for self-consumption by the agricultural producers themselves, the peasantry of Southeast Asia who form the vast majority of the population of the region.

The plight of the peasants has actually been worsened in many respects by "rural development" and "modernization." With population growth, the loss of natural resources, and increasing dependence on market forces, they are finding it more difficult than before to obtain enough food for their own subsistence. They find it necessary to sell their produce at the market price in order to pay their debts for the fertilizers, livestock, and other materials used in the production process. Many do not have enough produce left for their own consumption throughout the year and so have to buy food from the market, thus increasing their debts. Their problems are multiplied during years of drought or flooding. The trends are common throughout the region. The wealthy farmers with enough land to produce a surplus easily obtain bank loans to modernize their production and benefit from government support schemes. But they are a small minority of the rural population. The agribusinesses are also flourishing and gradually extending their operations to the more remote rural areas. They run their own farms or plantations through the use of hired laborers working at subsistence wages. While the farmers may receive higher incomes than before, these plantations place the farmers under their control and monopolize the markets in their areas of production. They also drive the small farmers further towards bankruptcy.

The vast majority of rural producers are the peasants with only sufficient land to feed their own families, the poor peasants with very small plots of land, the sharecropping tenants who lose up to half their produce as rent, and the agricultural laborers. They are finding it increasingly difficult to survive. They have no bargaining power concerning market prices, land rents, and daily wages. To obtain loans they have to resort to the local traders and money-lenders to whom they pay exorbitant interest rates. Their costs of production are increasing in comparison to the income they receive from their produce. The peasants of Southeast Asia are therefore plagued by mounting debts. In Thailand, for example, the five million rural families have accumulated a total of over US$1 billion while the average annual cash income per family is only US$170.

Under these conditions, it is not surprising that malnutrition is on the increase among the food producers and that a large proportion of rural families can no longer survive on agricultural production alone. The poor peasants are gradually losing their land thrugh debt, and millions of peasants flock to the cities each year to seek seasonal or year-round employment. The young girls work as servants or unskilled factory workers or are forced into prostitution. Children work illegally in small workshops under the harshest conditions. Some of them are even "sold" abroad. The men do heavy labor for low daily wages.

The massive influx of peasants to the cities clearly spotlights the misery of the rural population. Such migration to the cities does not solve the problem of rural poverty. Industry is not well enough developed to absorb the rural population. The workers from the rural areas receive barely sufficient wages for their own subsistence. Only a small proportion manage to send back money to their families. Living in the slum areas, they are faced with rising urban unemployment. Many are forced to resort to crime.

The worsening situation of the peasants has contributed to the growing strength of many underground revolutionary movements in the region. In retaliation, the governments have introduced repressive measures such as martial law, detention without trial, censorship, and violations of many fundamental human rights. Most of the Southeast Asian governments are military or military-backed authoritarian regimes. Under these conditions, the peasants are subject to atrocities and find it extremely difficult to join together to protect their common interests and struggle for their rights to a better time. Most farm organizations such as agricultural cooperatives and farmers unions are tightly controlled by the governments and mainly serve the interests of the wealthy farmers. When governments form a link like the Association of Southeast Asian Nations (ASEAN), they share repressive methods against the peasantry as well.

Women, who form half the work force of the region, have traditionally suffered from cultural repression. In the present age they are also the objects of extreme economic repression. They do the hardest work for the lowest wages. Millions are forced into semislavery, working as servants or prostitutes. The Southeast Asian sex market on which the tourist industries of the region thrive is famous throughout the world. Many of these women have also been "exported" to Europe, Hong Kong, and Japan.

The results of the rural development policies as implemented by the governments of Southeast Asia and supported by Japan and Western governments as well as international financial institutions have mainly been to widen the gap between the rich and the poor and to increase the misery of the rural populations for the benefit of the local elites and the wealthy societies of Japan and the West.

The situation as described above mainly applies to the countries of Southeast Asia under the ASEAN grouping (Thailand, Malaysia, Indonesia, and the Philippines). Although Singapore is a member of ASEAN, its peasant population is negligible. In Burma and the countries of Indochina, rural poverty is also prevalent, and in some areas the suffering of the peasants may be worse. The causes, however, are somewhat different. These countries are less "developed" than the ASEAN countries and are less tied to outside market forces. In some areas, the peasants are still producing mainly for self-consumption under the traditional community production system. But much of the peasantry has suffered enormously from wars and internal fighting that have plagued the region, appropriation of agricultural produce to support military growth, and mismanagement of internal market systems.

2. How the Southeast Asian governments have attempted to deal with rural poverty

As already mentioned, the main strategies for rural development implemented by the governments in Southeast Asia have been to extend and improve infrastructures, support the modernization of agricultural production, and encourage local and foreign investment in agriculture-related industries. In recent years, however, the problem of unequal distribution of benefits and the growing bankruptcy among the peasants has become widely recognized. Against a background of increasing discontent and armed struggle supported by a sizable number of peasants, the governments of the region have attempted to ease tensions by introducing reform program aimed directly at the rural poor. These programs have not, however, been effective in significantly increasing the distribution of wealth to the peasants as a whole, for three main reasons. First, without radically changing the economic systems of the Southeast Asia countries for the benefit of the majority of the population, reform measures cannot compete against the free-market forces that are the major cause of the hardships suffered by the peasants. At present the governments are only spending a minute proportion of the national budgets on agrarian reform (less than 1 percent in the Philippines, for example). Second, the governments of the region are based almost exclusively on the support of the wealthy and powerful sectors of society such as the military and the business community and cannot act against the interests of their own power base. Third, reform programs are implemented by bureaucracies of government officials more accustomed to governing than serving the peasants and with strong links to the local landlords, merchants, and businessmen. It is therefore not surprising that the peasants are not benefiting significantly from government reform programmes.

In those countries where land ownership is a major problem, land reform programs have been established with much heralding. In the present age, the traditional landlords are a slowly declining class, an obstacle to the modernization of agriculture and the expansion of agricultural businesses. Nevertheless, the land reform programs such as those established in the Philippines and Thailand are full of loopholes and are implemented at such a slow pace that only a small proportion of the peasants who were originally intended to benefit from the programs have actually received land rights. In the Philippines it is estimated that only about 13 percent of tenants and landless workers are eligible to benefit from the land reform programs. In the first seven years since the program was enacted, only one tenant in two hundred actually received a land ownership title.

Other measures carried out by Southeast Asian governments to help the rural poor have included sharecropping legislation, support for agricultural cooperatives and farmers' associations, price-support schemes, loan and debt-transfer schemes, rural employment programs, concentration of development funding on particularly deprived areas, and decentralization of development programs. In practice these measures have not been nearly as effective as intended, since they cannot overcome the system of unequal distribution of benefits. Agricultural cooperatives and farmers' associations have been inefficiently and corruptly managed and have mainly benefited the richer farmers. Poor farmers find it extremely difficult to obtain government loans due to the rigid conditions attached. Sharecropping legislation restricting land rents has been largely unenforceable in Indonesia and Thailand due to the influence of the landowners. Price support schemes mainly benefit the rich farmers and such middlemen as the rice-mill owners. Debt-transfer schemes do not work since most of the loans provided to the peasants are enforced by the power of the moneylenders. As for rural employment and local development programs, although the benefits do trickle down to the poor, they are planned and implemented by local powers and often enrich local officials and contractors.

Recently, the Thai and Malaysian governments have started to support community development programs at the village level. This is following the trend of development work carried out by some of the nongovernment organizations. The villagers are encouraged to develop their own communities by forming their own organizations, establishing their own development programs in consultation with local officials, and implementing the programs with financial and technical aid provided by the governments. If sufficient funds and expertise were available, and if community organization was implemented appropriately, this new strategy for the development of poor communities could go some way towards improving the lives of the rural poor. In practice, however, there are many obstacles to be overcome, and it is still too early to evaluate the results. A major limitation already apparent is that the aim of community development as established by the governments is to improve the material well-being of the communities rather than their social consciousness and political participation. Thus, the villagers are encouraged to create their own primary health-care schemes, establish drug cooperatives, improve their water resources, develop handicrafts, establish day-care centers for children, and so on. While these activities may help the villagers, they are not likely to seriously challenge the power structures and market forces which are at the root of the problems of the rural poor. Community organization and training is being carried out by local government officials who often do not understand the real meaning of community development and who are accustomed to giving orders rather than listening to the villagers. Nevertheless, the policy of supporting community organization and self-development is an important step in the right direction and may contribute to developments not anticipated by the governments concerned.

3. How the nongovernment organizations and peasant movements have attempted to alleviate rural poverty

Traditionally, peasant movements and struggles in Southeast Asia have been spontaneously formed, lacking leadership and direction. They have arisen from unbearable injustices suffered by the peasants and have been crushed by the authorities. One example is that of the local peasant associations and the Peasant Federation of Thailand that emerged during the period of relative political freedom between 1973 and 1976. During a period of three months in 1975, however, at least thirty of the peasant leaders throughout the country were assassinated. The Federation was abolished by the coup d'etat of October 1976.

Much more effective have been the underground revolutionary movements operating in the region with sizable numbers of peasants contributing to their forces. These movements have had a lasting effect in educating large sections of the population on the causes and structures behind rural poverty. They have shown how people's movements can challenge the existing power structures and have forced the authorities to implement rural reforms. The revolutionary movements themselves, however, have suffered to different extents from internal problems such as dogmatic ideology, leadership power struggles, and domination or interference by outside powers. Events in China and Indochina have led many people to question whether these movements, if successful, would in their present form bring about a better life for the peasants.

Political parties have made little contribution toward alleviating rural poverty. This is because the political parties that have been allowed to develop have been parties representing the rich and powerful.

Until recently, nongovernment organizations attempted to ease the suffering of the poor through individual handouts. These organizations were based on the western model of charities and denied any connections with politics. Today they have taken on a "development" approach. Instead of providing handouts to the poor, they train the poor to help themselves. They provide vocational training to the unemployed, teach handicrafts to the rural women, train village volunteers as health workers, and so on. Run by well-intentioned people, these organizations can ease some of the suffering of the poor. And yet, these voluntary agencies represent the interests of the rich, and their "development" operations are limited to supporting the material advancement of the poor under existing structures.

During the past ten years or so, a different kind of NGO has emerged, operated by church people, doctors, university lecturers, teachers, experienced field-workers, and other professionals. Even some Buddhist monks and Muslim leaders have been involved in this venture. Their main difference from traditional voluntary agencies is that their objective is to eliminate the source of rural poverty. They aim to raise the social consciousness and political participation of the poor, enabling the poor to eventually control their own destiny. These development groups are often regarded with suspicion by the authorities. Their activities may appear similar to the traditional voluntary agencies in that they may concentrate on specific areas of community development work such as community health, income development, child malnutrition, community leader-training programs, credit unions, and the like. It may still be necessary to enter rural communities with a "top-down" approach. This is often due to political restrictions. Under certain circumstances, however, it is possible for the development groups to directly implement community organization activities through the "bottom-up" approach.

The contributions made to the alleviation of rural poverty by such "progressive" development groups are very important. First, they can bring about the development of politically conscious peasant organizations at the local level. Second, they can inform the public about social problems and their causes, thus increasing public awareness and support and pressuring the authorities to implement further reforms. Third, they can form the basis for political action groups and political movements. These "progressive" development groups are plagued by many problems such as lack of experience, lack of coordination among themselves, lack of common direction, and dependence on funding from foreign sources.

At present the Philippines has the strongest formation of "progressive" NGO's. They have accumulated a good deal of experience and closely coordinate their work with political action groups and political movements. One of the main reasons for their strength has been the development of the progressive church movement as an impressive leading force for change which the authorities have found impossible to suppress. In Thailand and Malaysia, the "progressive" NGO's find it very difficult to operate due to rigid government control and suppression of opposition forces. In Burma some leading Buddhists and Protestant ministers have established significant development projects at local levels and have not yet been regarded as threats to the national government.

4. <u>How can rural poverty in Southeast Asia be successfully tackled?</u>

Obviously, to overcome rural poverty in Southeast Asia, the present economic systems and power structures will have to be changed to the advantage of the majority of the rural population. This does not mean returning to the traditional systems of agricultural production. The tide of modernization cannot be turned back. However, in order to bring about a better life for the peasants, market forces and economic growth will have to be carefully controlled so that the benefits reach the majority of producers. New systems of agricultural production and marketing must be implemented so that the peasants can control their own production and are no longer subservient to market forces. This can only be achieved through relentless struggle because the present governing powers, the local ruling elites backed by international forces, will not easily relinquish their economic and political power.

The supreme task of bringing about a better life for the peasants can be accomplished only through organization and cooperation. This must be the common task of all progressive forces in the Southeast Asian countries: political action groups, political movements, church organizations, trade unions, development organizations, community organizations, and others. In order to succeed, these organizations must work together in close coordination, having common goals and using appropriate methods learned through study and experience. In order to be able to organize properly, the peasants require better education and health services. It would not be appropriate to single out any particular type of organization or activity as the only solution to the liberation of the peasantry. The organizations must work together to create strong community organizations and peasant movements. All activities carried out towards this goal are implicitly political and will inevitably meet with resistance. Village scouts, self-defense volunteers, and other vigilante groups are being formed at the village level in order to fight against progressive forces. Community leaders are being assassinated. NGO's must develop appropriate tactics and methods of work to ensure the continuation of their activities. Through the consolidation of all progressive forces, there is hope for the long-term liberation of the peasants of Southeast Asia.

For those of us who struggle in the region, what is our solution? We simply could not wait for the monitoring of development in Asia, nor do we have any hope for a change to social justice through the political system prevailing in Asia. Yet there is no revolution around the corner, as our youth once seemed to believe. Indeed, socialist Vietnam, Laos, and Kampuchea do not have much to offer as an alternative to the capitalist system either.

We at ACFOD realize that the penetration of international capital into Asia has brought about militarization, violation of human rights of the people, and distortion of their cultural values, thereby accelerating the process of the rich becoming richer and the poor becoming poorer.

Through ACFOD, of which I happen to be the present coordinator, we try to face and help overcome these sad realities. Through our knowledge of Southeast Asian values inspired by or emanating from the region's religious and cultural heritage, members of ACFOD feel confident that we will succeed in solving some of the more fundamental problems.

ACFOD operates in Asia with headquarters located in Bangkok. It has been in operation since 1974. We have discovered many weaknesses in our programs; for instance, people's participation is still insufficient. We take courage in the fact that ours is perhaps the only regional nongovernment organization with grassroots participation.

The uniqueness of ACFOD lies in its utilization of the spiritual tradition and cultural values in development--a reinterpretation that adapts itself to the contemporary world. This has placed us in a position of challenging inadequate or even harmful models of development imposed by most Asian governments, which have a tendency to pay lip service to the spiritual tradition but in truth use it only for economic gains.

Duties of Life

"Quality of Life" from a Buddhist Perspective

Sulak Sivaraksa
ACFOD Coordinator

Prepared for World Council of Churches Pre-World Assembly Meeting in Mauritius, January 1983.

From a Buddhist world view, man is a unique being--above plants, animals, and other subhuman beings like ghosts and demons. But man is classified below other superior beings such as gods and angels. Yet man alone has potentiality to achieve the highest quality in life, the ultimate end of life cycle or liberation from sufferings.

Gods or angels have a much easier life than man, because they are so endowed with happiness that they do not realize that hatred, greed, and delusion still operate over them, consciously or subconsciously. Even if they do, it is not possible for them to exercise their spiritual strength to the degree that they could be liberated from their mode of existence. They could, of course, do a lot of good deeds, as well as do things harmful to themselves or to others.

One can say similar things about animals, especially the superior ones, like elephants, which can think very much like man and can develop such qualitative values as honesty, sincerity, and gratitude (even the wildest of the beasts can be tamed in such ways), but they can never overcome anger, lust, and ignorance.

In other words, the Buddhists regard man as a being who must have duties towards himself as well as towards all other beings in the whole environmental sphere; they believe that we are all fellow sufferers and we are all bound by birth, old age, sickness, and death. Whenever we confront things we do not like or have to depart from those we are fond of, we will suffer.

Whatever we can contribute to lessen suffering to ourselves as well as to others will be regarded as a good deed. All beings can make such a contribution. But only man has the ability not only to lessen suffering but also to eliminate the root cause of suffering entirely. Unless the root cause of suffering is eliminated, suffering will not be overcome.

It is therefore essential for man, if he wishes to take his duty seriously, to try to overcome or eliminate suffering. And the way to do this is laid down as a guideline by the Buddha. One does not need to declare oneself a Buddhist, but if one finds such a guide useful, one may study it and put it into practice.

For human development, from the Buddhist point of view, the first step is to take care of or to maintain physical growth. From the conception in the womb, the mother is asked to look after her baby's life as if it were her own. She should avoid certain foods as well as certain emotions which would endanger her baby's physical and mental well being. She is advised to meditate on loving-kindness so that the baby in her womb will develop spiritually. She is asked to offer food to monks daily so that the baby will be born with a charitable heart. She is also asked to keep the Buddhist five precepts regularly in order that the newly born will have a strong moral bent towards nonviolence, right means of livelihood, sexual restraint, truthfulness, and mindfulness.

Once a baby is born, he must be nurtured with the four essential requisites--food, clothing, shelter, and medicine--in order that he will grow up properly. There must not be too much food nor too little, and food is to preserve and nurture life, not to intoxicate it. The same rub is applied to other necessities. Clothing, for example, is to protect the body from the weather, not to exhibit the body or to show off how rich or important one is. Likewise with housing; it is only to protect one from the sun, the rain, and the wind. It is merely a place for one to dwell temporarily, not a place to show one's wealth, power, or prestige. When one is ill, one is required to take herbal medicine which, like food, must not be at the expense of some other being's livelihood. In order to develop one's life physically, one must also respect others.

Apart from depending on the four requisites, one is advised to have regular physical exercise. Yoga practice is very highly recommended so that physical fitness and proper physical growth can be maintained. Working in the field or using bodily strength is much encouraged, even at a tender age. But one must not do it beyond one's physical ability, nor should one do it in order to compete with others to show off one's superior physical energy, because this will endanger one's own physical growth and one's spiritual development. Sport is allowed only if it is a means for collaboration and for social unity. Sports which encourage competiton, violence, and gambling are very much condemned. Entertainment should also be for social well-being, not for a lustful end. For the Buddhists, without physical growth there will not be any human development of any kind. Yet physical development must be taken care of properly so that it will go along with one's social, spiritual, and intellectual growth. All these four are essential qualitative values of a human being.

In fact one should concentrate more on one's social growth than on one's physical growth, especially if one is not the poorest of the poor. The more one cares for others' physical and social growth, the more one will grow socially and spiritually.

Social growth in Buddhist terminology does not mean social recognition or socialization; it means that one cares about social justice--that is, one does not want to exploit oneself or others.

The basic rules for Buddhist morality are five. These are not commandments, but they are recommended for those who wish to have a social dimension to their human development.

They are

1. to abstain from killing.
2. to abstain from stealing.
3. to abstain from sexual misconduct.
4. to abstain from false speech.

5. to abstain from intoxicants causing heedlessness.

Practicing these five precepts, one is bound to be endowed with the five ennobling virtues, namely,

1. Loving-kindness and compassion
2. Right means of livelihood and generosity
3. Sexual restraint
4. Truthfulness and sincerity
5. Mindfulness and heedfulness

This pair of "fives" is essential to check a person's social growth. If he merely abstains from killing and stealing, yet puts his money into multinational corporations or international banks which exploit the poor and invest in armament businesses, he obviously lacks loving-kindness and his means of livelihood is certainly wrong.

Nowadays, a man may not commit adultery or tell lies, but if he uses sexual symbols to promote the sale of his goods, he is certainly not sincere. One only has to look at any advertisement in any of the mass media to see how social growth is lacking in the world. Even physical growth is, on the whole, badly maintained. The rich tend to eat too much and spend too much money on intoxicants and luxuries, while the majority suffer malnutrition and do not have adequate clothing and housing. The rich can also afford all kinds of medical treatment which can be very expensive, while most of the poor are treated by the "trained" medical profession as if they were subhuman. This is indeed social degradation, not social growth at all.

In order to achieve physical and social growth, one must develop the spiritual dimension simultaneously with the others; otherwise one is easily conceited and thinks that he has done his best already for himself and for others. It is therefore not surprising that members of the younger generation rebel against their own fathers, despite the fact that fathers claim they have done everything possible for their family.

To grow spiritually, first of all, one has to be calm and impartial so that he can find out what sort of a person he is. On the whole, one does not know or admit that he is lustful or greedy, even if he would like to become rich at the expense of others. If one lacks that negative quality, one is normally ambitious and would like to play with power--in the name of social justice or serving the poor. Beyond this, one is fairly ignorant about oneself as well as about the world in which one would normally dare to be involved and claim that one would solve those worldly problems.

One tends to know or to think of one's positive qualities only. Thus one feels hurt when people are not grateful for a generous deed one has done for them. One is angry when he is deceived, thinking he himself has been sincere and honest all the time. Furthermore, one feels that he has been good and hard-working but is not rewarded sufficiently, while crooked and second-rate people seem to do very well in the world.

All these symptoms show that one is not calm. Hence one has not penetrated inwardly to find out what is one's spiritual strength and weakness, what one should overcome, and what one should strengthen.

In Buddhism, meditation or mindfulness is essential for spiritual development. There are many techniques for teaching one to sit still, to be calm, alert, and awake from selfishness and self-conceit.

Once one knows his own ego and finds out how false it is to cling to it, one would have a prescription to restructure his consciousness in order to grow spiritually. Spiritual development can be trained in two steps. First of all, one must train oneself to be tranquil so as to be impartial. Then one can develop spiritual exercises by various insight development methods that lead to spiritual attainment. Those who practice this will eventually reach the First Absorption, which includes Thought Formation, Discursive Thinking, Rapture, Happiness, and Even-mindedness. They must, however, abandon this attainment and concentrate their mind until they reach the Second Absorption, which drops Thought Formation and Discursive Thinking. It is very difficult to have a proper Thought Formation and Discursive Thinking objectively. Yet, having been able to achieve the, one must abandon them for one's spiritual growth. Then, in order to achieve the Third Absorption, one must also be able to abandon spiritual Rapture; to reach the Fourth and final Absorption, one must not even cling to happiness. One will only dwell on Equanimity and Even-mindedness or One-pointedness.

What I have said so far may sound rather technical. For the noninitiated, to understand the difference between Rapture and Happiness is already difficult--not to mention Thought Formation and Discursive Thinking.

Hui-Neng, the Chinese sixth Patriarch of the Zen tradition, had this to say: "To know our mind is to obtain liberation. To obtain liberation is to attain Samadhi of Prajna, which is 'thoughtlessness.' What is 'thoughtlessness'? 'Thoughtlessness' is to see and to know all dharmas (things) with a mind free from attachment. When in use it pervades everywhere, and yet it sticks nowhere. What we have to do is to purify our mind so that the six vijnanas (aspects of consciousness) in passing through the six gates (sense organs) will neither be defiled by nor attached to the six sense-objects. When our mind works freely without any hindrance, and is at liberty to 'come' or'go', we attain Samadhi of Prajna, or liberation. Such a state is called the function of 'thoughtlessness.' But to refrain from thinking of anything, so that all thoughts are suppressed, is to be Dharma-ridden, and this is an erroneous view."

Let me quote from another Mahayana Sutra, the Dharma-sangiti, which said:

> The man whose mind is wrapt in meditation sees things as they are. The Bodhisattva who thus sees things as they are feels profound pity towards all beings; and thus he thinks: 'This meditation, the means, with the power of seeing all things as they are, I must put within the reach of all beings.' He being impelled by that profound pity towards lofty virtue, lofty thought, lofty wisdom--a

discipline fine in its fullness--attains full and perfect enlightenment. In essence, spiritual development is a means to cleanse the mind so that it would be calm and impartial. Once one has less self-interest, one will be ready for Intellectual Growth in its fullest sense of the word.

Intellectual Growth here does not mean that one is clever or brainy; rather, it has the sense of Gnostic or Wisdom, that is, one sees things as they really are. In other words, only through wisdom can one synchronize one's brain or one's mind with one's heart. It is not difficult intellectually to argue that to exploit the poor is bad but through Spiritual and Intellectual Development in this way, could one be convinced once and for all how not to exploit others in every variety of devious ways. One does not use any theory, ideology, preconceived idea, or selfish motive to tackle any situation.

From the Buddhist point of view, development must aim at the reduction of craving, the avoidance of violence, and the development of the spirit rather than of material things. As each individual progresses, he increasingly helps others without waiting for the millennium or for the ideal socialist society. Cooperation is better than competition, whether of the capitalist variety or of the socialist variety which favors the laborer.

From the standpoint of Buddhism, the goal can be attained by stages as evil desires are overcome. So goals are perceived in two ways. From the worldly standpoint, the more desires are increased or satisfied, the further development can proceed.

Western civilization erodes Christianity, or at least real Christian spiritual values, and becomes merely capitalistic or socialistic, aiming to increase material goods in order to satisfy craving. The capitalist variety wants to raise the material standard of living of other groups, if possible, provided the capitalists themselves can stay on top. The socialist variety reverses it and wants the majority, or those who act in the name of the majority, to oppress the minority or those who oppose the majority.

The value scale of Western-type development emphasizes extremes. The richer the better; capitalists apply this to the wealthy, socialists to the laborer. The quicker the better. The bigger the better. The more knowledge the better. Buddhism, on the other hand, emphasizes the middle way between extremes, a moderation which strikes a balance appropriate to the balance of nature itself. Knowledge must be a complete knowledge of nature in order to be wisdom; otherwise, knowledge is ignorance. Partial knowledge leads to delusion and encourages the growth of greed and hate. These are the roots of evil that lead to ruin. The remedy is the threefold way of self-knowledge, leading to right speech and action and right relations to people and things (morality), consideration of the inner truth of one's own spirit and of nature (meditation), leading finally to enlightenment or complete knowledge (wisdom). It is an awakening, a complete awareness of the world. When one understands this, one understands the three characteristics of all things from the Buddhist point of view: their unsatisfactoriness or suffering, their impermanence, and their lack of a permanent selfhood or ego.

True development will arrange for the rhythm of life and movement to be in accordance with the facts, while maintaining an awareness that man is but a part of the universe and that ways must be found to integrate mankind with the laws of nature. There must be no boasting, no proud or self-centered attempts to master nature, no emphasis placed on the creation of material things to the point where people become slaves to things and have no time left to search after the truth which is beyond the realm of material things.

In 1929, Max Scheler formulated a remark which is just as true today as then. He said,

> We have never before seriously faced the question whether the entire development of Western civilization, that one-sided and overactive process of expansion outward, might not ultimately be an

attempt using unsuitable means--if we lose sight of the complementary art of inner self-control over our entire underdeveloped and otherwise involuntary psychological life, an art of meditation, search of soul, and forbearance. We must learn anew to envisage the great invisible solidarity of all living beings in universal life, of all minds in the eternal spirit--and at the same time the mutual solidarity of the world process and the destiny of its supreme principle, and we must not just accept this world unity as a mere doctrine, but practice and promote it in our inner and outer lives.

This is indeed the spirit of Buddhist development, where inner strength must be cultivated first; then compassion and loving-kindness to others become possible. Work and play would be interchangeable. There is no need to regard work as something which has to be done, has to be bargained for, in order to get more wages or more leisure time. The Work ethic would not be to get ahead of others but to enjoy one's work and to work in harmony with others. Materially there may not be too much to boast about, but the simple life ought to be comfortable enough, and simple food is less harmful to the body and mind. Besides, a simple diet could be produced without exploiting nature, and one would then not need to keep animals merely for the sake of man's food.

Such is indeed the quality of life from the Buddhist perspective. For the Buddhist, physical, social, spiritual, and intellectual growth must be developed side by side, and they must all go toward the ultimate End of Liberation from all Sufferings.

The more modest we are, and the more simple our life style is, more it is possible for our physical growth in the proper sense of the word to go side by side with our own social development as well as with the social and physical development of the majority. If our lives were less complicated, we would have more time to meditate so that we would be calm and be able to develop insight for Absorption, and then we would have enough spiritual strength to pave the way for wisdom, since it is only through wisdom that hatred, greed, and delusion will be eliminated. As the Buddha put it, we all must have wisdom as our goal so that a wise man can eliminate his selfishness in order that he would be compassionate enough to serve all beings--human as well as nonhuman.

To be a true Buddhist, one must lead one's life in harmony with all others in the universe, by exploiting none and serving all. Yet one must serve mankind as well as others knowingly--not blindly. It really is one's duty to strive toward this fulfillment; otherwise one cannot say that one fully lives as a true human being.

VII

EPILOGUE AND CONCLUSION

The sixties and seventies have seen the emergence of religious movements for economic justice and change, networks of protest, and reform groups. These have become a significant characteristic of the cultural situation in South and Southeast Asia. The four movements we have sampled are part of this phenomenon. They reveal various degrees of disjuncture with present-day power structures and exemplify the religious influences that have contributed to this disjuncture. Some of these groups have informal relationships with governmental and international organizations; others are alienated from any such structures of power, working instead at the grass-roots level in the village. In some cases, they also consciously attempt to establish an alternative social and economic order.

Sarvodaya rejects collaborating with political parties as an avenue to influencing social decision, but has increasingly cooperated with the national government on some village projects. ACFOD has tenuous relations with authorities in Thailand, where it is headquartered, yet works with FAO and a variety of international agencies. The Christian Workers Fellowship has been subjected to government surveillance, and some staff members have been beaten and jailed for short times. TICD, perhaps the smallest of the movements considered, has managed to focus mainly on problems of Buddhism and village development in small but creative projects. Although it shares many concerns with the other three groups, it has not faced political opposition or been as involved in confrontation. The Christian Workers Fellowship has most directly confronted what it considers unjust power. It has used participation in strikes, public demonstrations, and support for minority rights among its methods of work. ACFOD, because of its internationally and politically inclusive leadership, is able to articulate macrocriticisms that generate an uneasy relationship with the power structures of particular countries.

Two major crises have confronted the movements studied since the original field work in 1982-83. Sulak Sivaraksa, the coordinator of ACFOD, was brought to trial on the charge of lese majeste. In Sri Lanka, Sarvodaya and CWF have been tested by a major outbreak of violence between the Sinhalese and the Tamil minority.

The Arrest and Trial of Sulak Sivaraksa

During the last several years the military and the right wing in Thailand have been jockeying to gain full political power. In March 1983 the military attempted to amend the constitution to allow senior military officials to concurrently hold high political office. Widespread protests by students, intellectuals, and human rights groups eventually led to the defeat of the amendment. However, it seemed clear that the military was not about to relax its drive for greater power. One method it has used in the power struggle has been to focus public attention on "communists" or other dissidents and to seek official and public support by using them as scapegoats. This method draws attention to the national symbolism of the military and attempts to diminish support for other factions in the government. In July of 1984 the special police of the Internal Security Operations Command arrested nineteen communist suspects, a university lecturer, and a newspaper editor on charges of assisting the communists.

On July 17 the director-general of the police department announced that more arrests would be made. On the same day, over a thousand copies of a book by Sulak Sivaraksa were confiscated by the police. The book, Lokkrab Sangkam Thai (Unmasking Thai Society), was alleged to undermine public order and morale. At the time of the confiscation, Sulak was in Japan participating in a Pacific Youth Forum sponsored jointly by ACFOD and the United Nations University.

He returned home as planned on July 26. On July 31 he went to the ACFOD office as usual, then had his hair cut before going to Thammasat University to give a public lecture entitled "Youth and Buddhism". When he arrived at the Political Science Auditorium, he was told that the special branch police were waiting for him at his home and had shown a warrant for his arrest to his son. He gave the lecture as planned but cut short the question period, telling the audience he was about to be arrested. He pleaded that there be no student demonstrations on his behalf. He felt that some of those aspiring to power or in power would exploit any conflict between the right wing and "left-wing" students. Some of his friends who had close contact with the military warned him not to go home and give in to arrest. They had heard rumors that there would be a coup late that evening and that the charges against him would be changed to being a communist suspect. It was thought that this charge would incite the students' anger. It was on such advice that Sulak hid for five days. On Sunday, August 5, he consulted his lawyer as to whether--and if so, when--he should give himself up. During his discussion with his lawyer he was arrested. Although it is still not known who initiated the arrest, the supposition is that military authorities and a right-wing group called the Village Scouts were immediately responsible. About a thousand Village Scouts massed at the Governmental House on July 28 to submit a letter to the deputy director-general of the police alleging that Sulak had made derogatory statements about the monarch in his recent book.

At first, bail was refused by the police, but on August 10 the chief justice of the criminal court granted him bail and he returned home.

Bail was extended several times into September and October. On September 26 the public prosecutor submitted his case to the military court, and hearings were scheduled for early in November. On November 8 Sulak heard unofficially that his case would be withdrawn from the court, although the political situation was tense and uncertain. From November 26 to 30 he participated in a World Council of Churches conference in Singapore on development and justice. On the twenty-seventh he was called to return home immediately to appear in court, but he refused.

"They kept me waiting for so long. Now they might as well wait for me a little," he wrote.[1]. After completing his participation in the conference on December 29, he flew back to Bangkok and went to court on the thirtieth. The presiding judge informed him that the public prosecutors had asked the court to have the case withdrawn. Never before in Thai history had a case based on lese majeste been withdrawn from court. His lawyer, Mr. Thongpai Thongpoo, went straight from the courtroom to an ASEAN conference on human rights then taking place at Thammasat University and announced the outcome. There was great jubilation, and Mr. Thongpai was elected president of the Regional Council on Human Rights in Asia.

Undoubtedly one reason for the withdrawal of the case was widespread international protest by letter and cable and inquiries by foreign governments as to the disposition of the case. Petitions by international groups of Thai scholars, United Nations University, and many of Sulak's friends in universities and nongovernmental organizations had some impact. Sulak still has to be careful, for dissidents like him have suffered bodily harm.

During this period of personal and legal turmoil, Sulak said he reflected on the words of M. M. Thomas, a well-known Indian Christian:

> Nationalism--with its emphasis on national security, unity and stability, tends to become an ethos for preserving the structure against change, and to justify the suppression of democratic rights and mass action for change . . . The struggle for social justice is the transformation of existing structures of state, economic order and society, so that the poor and oppressed may become full participants in the total life of society.[2]

The Sinhala-Tamil Conflict--July 1983

"We are in the midst of our worst national crisis since the regaining of our independence." So wrote Bishop Lakshman, Anglican bishop and founding member of the Christian Workers Fellowship, in his anguished final pastoral letter before his death on Sunday, October 23, 1983. In the letter, entitled "A Cry From the Heart," the bishop bemoaned the irrational passions which between July 23 and July 31 of that year had led to orgies of riots, murders, assaults, and beatings. On July 23, in the midst of repression, an armed group of Tamils had attacked an army patrol in the Jaffra peninsula in northern Sri Lanka, killing thirteen soldiers. Frustrated in its attempts to punish those responsible, the army killed more than seventy civilians in counterassaults. Part of the mainly Sinhalese crowd attending the soldiers' funeral in Colombo broke into gangs that went on rampages in the Tamil sections of the city. Sinhalese mobs in other sections of the country followed suit. The government's estimate of the casualties was 1,500 murders and 150,000 left homeless. Vast areas of stores and houses in Tamil sections were burned.

The tension between Tamils and Sinhalese is unfortunately of long standing. Ancient Tamil kings had been fought and eventually repulsed or held in check. For a considerable time Indian Tamils occupied the northern sections of the island. The history of ancient Sri Lanka demonstrates the intertwining of Tamil culture with that of the Sinhalese. As Professor Bardwell Smith comments:

> One thread which provides both meaning and threat to Sinhalese self-consciousness is the ever-recurring pressure of Tamil invasion and occupation. Neither the present scene in Ceylon nor its lengthy history can be understood without a vivid awareness of the ambivalent relationship between these two peoples, now one of alliance and reciprocity, now of embittered hostility. Over the centuries it was essentially the latter with prevailed.[3]

From the Tamil perspective, the Tamils have been a self-governing people during different periods of their long history. Both the Tamils and the Sinhalese had lost their sovereignty due to foreign invasions since the sixteenth century. In modern times the British brought in Tamil laborers from India to work the tea plantations in central Sri Lanka. The plantation workers of recent Indian origin do not have the same sense of nationalism as the Tamils who have been in Sri Lanka for centuries. The Sinhalese feel that some of this "foreign labor" has come to live and work on some of the best agricultural land. Because of their resentment, about a quarter million Tamils have been repatriated to India.

Recent tension stems from a demand by a faction of the Tamils for a division of the island providing for a separate Tamil state. Many Tamils think that a point of no return has been reached and that a political division is the only way to defuse further tensions. Some Sinhalese, on the other hand, see total assimilation of Tamils, culturally and linguistically, as the only way to attain a unified nation.

The overt conflicts have been going on at least since 1951-1952, when plantation workers and some other Ceylonese Indians staged a Satyagraha campaign to protest their decitizenization and disenfranchisement under post-Independence citizenship laws. The campaign was short-lived, but disenfranchisement left wounds that have not healed.

In 1948-1949, the school system was separated into three: Sinhala, Tamil, and English. In the 1950s English was forced out of the schools. The segregation of children according to the language of instruction tends to heighten ethnic tensions.

Another communal conflict came with the Tamil protests against the "Sinhala Only Act" in 1956. Sinhala was made the official language of government, immediately putting the Tamils at a disadvantage. Unequal language requirements denied access to legal and public services and to promotional opportunities with government service. The Tamil Federal Party became the chief spokesman for the Tamils in the late nineteen fifties. It succeeded in gaining agreements with prime ministers Bandaraniake in 1957 and Senanayake in 1965. Recognition was granted by legislation in 1958 and 1966 for greater use of Tamil in regional government affairs. However, the complaint remains that these legislative actions have been poorly implemented. As a result of the disturbed Sinhalese-Tamil relations there were bloody riots in 1958. In the spring of 1961 there were massive civil disobedience campaigns in the northern and eastern provinces directed against the language policies of Mrs. Bandaranaike's administration. In October, 1964, prime minister Bandaranaike concluded a pact with India known as the "Srima-Shastri Pact". India agreed to take back 525,000 persons and Ceylon was to grant citizenship to 300,000 persons of Indian origin. The agreement was to be implemented by October, 1979. However this period has been extended. Although the insurrection of 1971 was primarily not an ethnic conflict, one of its results was the introduction of terrorism and armed struggle to the Tamil areas of the north.[4].

By the mid-1970s there were articulate Tamil demands for a separate Tamil state. The Tamil United Liberation Front affirmed, by the Vaddukoddai Resolution on May 14, 1976, the goal of setting up "a separate, free, secular, sovereign socialist state of Tamil Eelam [Ceylon]."[5]

During the 1977 general election the United National Party appealed for national unity and pledged to remedy Tamil grievances in education, employment, and use of language.

Violence against the Tamils was again unleashed in August 1977. As a result there were about fifty thousand refugees in several camps in a number of cities. Plantation workers were also attacked. (This period was discussed earlier in connection with the CWF work on the tea plantations.)

The Sarvodaya Movement's Reaction to the Crisis

The years of unrest, particularly in the north, were brought to a head by the uncontrolled violence of July 1983--a crisis of national identity. Most religious leaders in the nation recognized that far more profound measures needed to be taken to address the national crisis.

The Sarvodaya movement took a very active role in establishing a refugee camp in Colombo at the Ratmalana airport just north of the city. At one point about five thousand persons were served at this center. Ariyaratne and others walked the streets in the nearby Wellawatte area offering assistance, particularly to homeless children.

A "People's Declaration for National Peace and Harmony" was one result of a general conference called at the invitation of Sarvodaya on October 1 and 2 at the International Conference Hall in Colombo.

This conference began a searching analysis of the role of the movement in Tamil-Sinhala relationships, raising comprehensive questions for more detailed investigation. The conference agreed on the deficiency of an educational system that assumed the value of a "competitive commercial human society" and the "waning influence of monks."[6]. The declaration echoed many of the criticisms of the social order in earlier Sarvodaya statements. (See pp. 51 - 55) Interestingly, the statement harks back to Sarvodaya's philosophy of a partyless political order. It advocated the creation "without any further delay [of] an alternative political system in keeping with our values and needs, in place of the party-based system which is a western product, and is one of the primary causes of the degeneration of and the many ills evident in present day society.. . ."[7].

There has been and continues to be some soul searching in Sarvodaya about its relationship to the Tamil people.

One potentially valuable offshoot of the international conference was a proposed "peace walk" from Kataragama in the south to Point Pedro in the north. The aim of the walk was to generate a common consciousness of religious and moral values and to encourage respect for human rights and justice. The walk recruited one hundred persons selected and led by A.T. Ariyaratne. They pledged themselves to a nonviolent discipline similar to that of the Gandhian protest marches in India. Numerous community activities and educational programs were planned to encourage interethnic understanding. The walk was planned to take 118 days and end in Jaffna.

The walk had barely begun when on the personal appeal of Prime Minister Jayewardene it was called off. The prime minister was fearful of violence, and especially of rumored danger to Ariyaratne. The fact that the appeal came from the prime minister personally and had a note of urgency about it was enough to halt the march. Ariyaratne yielded in his determination to carry through the march when he realized he might put others in danger.

Sarvodaya is a Buddhist-motivated movement that has successfully worked out a program of village development and through self-reliance. The movement's research director, in an evaluation in 1977, recognized that in the early 1970s the Sri Lankan Tamil participation in the Sarvodaya Shramadana Movement was only about 5 1/2 percent of its total and Indian Tamils less than 1 percent. The Sri Lankan population as a whole is 11 percent Sri Lankan Tamil and 9 percent Indian Tamils. At that time, Dr. Ratnapala indicated that the movement "has not moved in a tangible way and taken root among non-Sinhalese-speaking people as one would wish it to be. Although in recent times a number of Tamil Hindu villages in the north and Muslim/Malay villages in the south have joined the movement, there are sociocultural factors which retard its quick spread among ethnic groups, other than the Sinhalese."[8].

The movement is sensitive to Hindu religious traditions, as Joanna Macy reports. Hindu religious hymns and rituals are incorporated into family gatherings in Tamil areas. In Jaffna it is the Indian Sarvodaya ideal of Vinoba Bhave and Gandhi that are practically followed.[9].

Sarvodaya has encouraged Tamil and Sinhalese students and participants in the movement to exchange family visits and to study each other's languages.

S. Pamarasingam offered an insightful view of Sarvodaya Shramadana village work in the light of the July 1983 crisis. In a paper presented to the Sri Lanka Foundation Institute, he wrote:

> I must say that I have been impressed by what I have seen in the Sarvodaya Village Centres in Sinhalese, Tamil and Muslim areas--there are over 6,000 of them so far--in all parts of the country. The Sarvodaya village is based on the Gandhian concept of the traditional society of a multi-level, multi-faceted character based on tolerance and interdependence. What Sarvodaya wants to do like Sarvodaya in India, is not to provide an alternative to what British and its present-day allies have sought to build in our villages, but to leap-frog over that rather weak and uncertain superstructure that had been imposed on them into a new society based on the spirit of old interdependent traditional village tolerance. The old spirit still exists, but it has to be given new form and content to suit contemporary times.[10]

The Christian Workers Fellowship Response

The response of the CWF to the role of political parties after the July 1983 crisis was somewhat different from that of Sarvodaya's response. The government proscribed three political parties due to the emergency--the Janata Vimukthi Peramuna (JVP), the Communist Party of Sri Lanka (CPSL), and the Nara Sama Samaja Party (NSSP). The CWF, even though most of its members are unlikely to be members of these groups, protested the government action. It called for the government either to make known any reasons why these parties should be prohibited or to permit them to function again. CWF views the free functioning of political parties as necessary for the proper functioning of democracy. It will be recalled that Sarvodaya has decried "the party- and power-oriented political system" and seeks its replacement by "an alternate democratic system of administration."[11]

In the <u>Christian Worker</u> the editor commented: "As we have said before in these columns, even if a genuine end to racism as to other social ills has to await a future socialist reconstruction of society, a method of co-existence must be found in the meantime if we are to avoid complete disaster as a people."[12]. In the same statement the editor called for decentralization of power throughout the country to effect a greater democratization by having elected representatives of local units develop and administer their own areas[13].

The CWF center in Ratmalana, near Colombo, helped shelter refugees during the first days of the July rioting. The main item on the agenda of the Hatton center was relief and rehabilitation work among victims of racial disturbances in the plantation areas near Hatton, Nawalapitiya, and Pussellawa. CWF workers took clothing and dry rations to 1,350 rubber workers in Yatiyantota. The Rural Service Center in Galaha helped authorities patrol the area with volunteers to assist in maintaining peace. In Badulla a young CWF group helped collect food and clothes for refugees at a nearby rehabilitation camp.

Among others indiscriminately arrested after the July violence were, Jeffrey Abayasekera and Annathgail Abayasekera, husband and wife, who serve the Hatton Center. They were detained by the police in Hatton and Peradenyia for two weeks in September. Files, CWF publications, and minutes of meetings were taken with them from their residence, which also serves as the CWF's Hatton center. Apparently the police suspected CWF of subversion, even though their pamphlets and publications clearly demonstrate a strong stand against terrorism and racial violence.

The main thrust of the movements we have studied is economic justice for the poor, particularly the rural poor. However, recent events amply demonstrate that such movements inevitably become involved in ethnic tensions, civil rights issues, and political controversy. Their staying power and effectiveness have depended--and will depend--on their ability to cope with a broad spectrum of issues and crises in their societies and on the religious vision which undergirds their efforts.

Relationships to Buddhism

Three of the four movements studied are deeply influenced by Buddhist traditions. The Asian Cultural Forum on Development is indeed interfaith in purpose and organization. Early in its development it was decided not to include the word "religion" in its organizational name. However, since its coordinator is a leading Buddhist layman and its headquarters is in Bangkok, Buddhism provides one important influence on its development. The Thai Inter-Religious Committee on Development has Catholic board members and participants, but the young people who are the body of the movement are Buddhist. Buddhatat's writing and thought provide the central intellectual and religious focus for the group. It is interesting to note that Buddhatat's interpretations draw on Mahayana Buddhist thought, chiefly Zen, as well as reasserting a classical dharmic foundation. Sarvodaya Shramadana has been the most articulate in its advocacy of the Buddhist dharma and has made Buddhism an integral part of its program in village reconstruction and self-help. As it has moved into Tamil and Christian areas Sarvodaya has been sensitive in broadening its ideological base and to avoid chauvinistic nationalism. Ariyaratne, in some of his recent addresses, seems to avoid using religious terminology in order not to stir up ethnic antagonism. The scholarship and insights of Walpola Rahula, Buddhatat, Phra Rajavaramuni, David Kalupahana and the late K. N. Jayatillike have played an important part in informing the various groups.

At the level of ritual and practice, the family gatherings that are central to the Shramadana work camps have the most marked religious element of any of the three Buddhist influenced movements. Customarily the Triple refuge and the Five precepts are recited. A period of silent meditation is a regular part of family gatherings as well as part of the daily observance at Sarvodaya Headquarters in Colombo.

TICD has had its participants practice insight meditation at Buddhatat's Wat at Suan Mok. His teaching on meditation has been discussed in Chapter V. The chief ritual related activity is their reinterpretation of the Rice Papha ceremony described in some detail in the reading following Chapter V.

ACFOD as an organization has not engaged in any religious ritual other than memorial services for its past Coordinator.

All of the movements considered engage in educational and community self-help program with Buddhist monks. Sarvodaya has its own impressive Bhikkhu training center. Monks are present in many of its activities and play an important role in beginning many Shramadana work camps. Joanna Macy suggests that they may not be as much in evidence as when the movement was first initiating projects in Sri Lanka. Sarvodaya's own self-evaluation is that the Bhikkhu training program needs to improve its recruitment of student monks and the effectiveness of its teaching staff.

TICD's main effort has been workshops and training programs with Thai Bhikku's. They have supported monks participation in community reconstruction and development projects in a number of wats in various sections of the country. They are also giving attention to research and projects to deal with the urgent problems of urban wats in the Bangkok megalopolis.

Buddhism and Economic Justice

What is the Buddhist foundation for economic ethics? The leaders of ACFOD, TICD and Sarvodaya Shramadana all call on the Buddhist tradition as a source of socio-economic criticism. It is important, therefore, to briefly summarize their views of Buddhist economic ethics.

Ethical or moral causality has a central place in early Buddhist teachings. Moral responsibility (<u>sila</u>), concentration (<u>samadhi</u>), and wisdom (<u>panna</u>) are three divisions of the eightfold path, the way to enlightenment or liberation. At the core of Buddhist ethics and the early monastic order is respect for and benevolence toward all lives. In the <u>Kassapasihanda Sutta</u> the true meditator or monk is he who cultivates universal benevolence and expresses toward all beings. As Ariyaratne describes it:

> If the motivating force in the mind is Metta or respect for all lives then a human being who accepts this principle has to necessarily translate this thought into concrete compassionate action called 'karuna' . . . we are helping a landless cultivator to liberate himself from the bondage imposed on him by unscrupulous landowners not because we hate the landowner but because we love and respect the life of the poor landless cultivator.[14]

While some distinction may be made between early Buddhist ethics for the ordinary person and the more extraordinary ethics for monastics, metta and karuna apply to everyone.

Also, as Tambiah has pointed out, the Sangha [or brotherhood of monks] demonstrates Gautama Buddha's concern to establish a new community. The Buddhist Sangha is socially significant because it brought together all strata of society on an equal footing in worship and organization.[15] The begging bowl of the monks became a symbol of the interdependence of all persons since the acceptance of food from persons regardless of caste was now a rule of the order. This was a rejection of the Hindu social-metaphysical dharma. Gautama views the new community or sangha as a means of affecting the well being of society as a whole. "Go wander for the happiness of many," is his injunction (bahujanahitaya bahujanasukkhaya). He addresses the social ethics of lay society in teaching reciprocal duties of workers and employers, students and teachers, children and parents. It is thought that Gautama was responding to a changing and more urbanizing social structure. The early Buddhist tradition by no means lacks specific economic ethics. The Cakkravarti Sutta describes the decline in society because the needs of the poor are not attended to by the king. Gautama is reported to have taught that the hungry need to be fed in order that they may understand the moral law or teaching (dharma). The ideal society or kingdom in the Maha-Sudassana-Sutta is described as one in which food, raiment and transportation is available for those in need. In the Agganna-Sutta the cause of hunger is said to be the unjust practice of the wealthy adding numerous rice fields to their holdings.

Sulak Sivaraksa of ACFOD interprets the Buddhist concern for the poor:

> The more one cares for others physical and social growth, the more one will grow socially and spiritually. Social growth in Buddhist terminology does not mean social recognition or socialization, but it means that one cares about social justice--that is one does not want to exploit oneself or others.[16]

"Quality of Life" from a Buddhist perspective according to Sulak, depends on four requisites: food, clothing, shelter and medicine. Physical development must be taken care of properly so that it will coincide with social, spiritual and intellectual growth. Sarvodaya in formulating the list of "Ten Basic Human Needs" (quoted in Chapter III) also builds on the base of physical well being and adds educational, cultural and spiritual development.

As Joanna Macy interprets the Vyaggha and Kutadanta sutras there is a striking alternative to classical Western economics. "From the perspective of the Dharma, economic interest includes not only production and profit, but also the 'externalities' of human and environmental costs. The conservation of material resources, their humane use, and their equitable distribution are taken as legitimate and indeed preeminent concerns."[17]

Two issues can be raised in the above interpretations of Buddhist ethics. First, while the early Buddhist sources provide a rich source for constructing an economic ethnic suited to modern society some would emphasize that this is a modern reconstruction or reconception. There is always the problem of a too facile modernization. Present day interpretations have to be concerned for change at an institutional or infrastructural level. Such concerns were not part of early

Buddhist ethics. Secondly, it may be argued that the movements and their leaders are only using Buddhist terms and symbols in a pragmatic way to enlist support for their organizations. That may be partly true. Buddhism itself sometimes is interpreted as a very pragmatic religion.

However, the leaders of the movement investigated have been consistent over the years in presenting Buddhist ethics. They have shown openness and great interest in working with Buddhist scholars. One senses a genuine depth of reflection on their Buddhist faith.

Religion and the Social Vision

The interaction of religion and social criticism has been a recurring theme in this study. A dialectic is at work in these movements between focusing on particular religious traditions and addressing a larger interregional or international constituency. To some extent they seek approval or validation, along with financial backing, from the larger international community. However, the social vision of these movements has been and is social justice. That focus, whether motivated by Christian or Buddhist religious connections, gives these movements a sharper cutting edge in their societies than churches or temples whose purposes are more diffuse.

To briefly summarize the vision of the four movements:

1. All give normative priority to economic justice, particularly distributional justice in relation to the rural poor.
2. They identify with those that are economically and ethnically marginalized. This identification comes through practical self-help projects and through political action.
3. They seek changes in the economic structure of society. Sarvodaya emphasizes self-reliant villages. The Christian Workers Fellowship advocates "indigenous Marxist socialism."
4. They stress empowerment of decision making at the village or local level.

5. Religious faith is a primary resource and chief motivational factor in transforming the social order.

The movements we have studied are all responses to the inequalities of fortune, primarily of the rural poor--landless laborers and small farmers, fishers, and plantation workers. Although the movements exist to serve those at the margins of the economic system, they also provide a way of relating the poor to the middle class and to some religious leaders in society. Although only TICD makes explicit its role in sensitizing the middle class to the needs of the poor, all the groups serve that purpose.

ACFOD is the most secular and at the same time the most inclusive group. Although ACFOD affirms the importance of religious communities and traditions, they set these alongside other purposes in their programs. An international network like ACFOD, which is intentionally pluralistic and politically and religiously inclusive, will always work within the dialectic of meeting particular grass-roots needs and determining policy and program at an international level. When ACFOD's leaders operate within the Thai context they talk in Buddhist terms, but at ACFOD council meetings their deliberations have to include Catholics, Muslims, and Marxists.

Sarvodaya's purposes and ethical affirmations are largely within the Buddhist world view. Indeed, its success is that it was able in its early years to take Gandhian, European, and secular influences and transform them into a Sri Lankan Buddhist ethos. Now, as the largest Buddhist movement concerned with economic justice in the third world, it must appraise its achievements and limitations in reaching across ethnic and religious lines. As we have seen, Sarvodaya has been critical of its own limited ability to work in Tamil areas.

The Role of Religious Leaders

The engaging personality and inspiring social vision of Anglican bishop Lakshman Wickremesinghe and Catholic bishop Leo Nanayakkara were important in the development of the Christian Workers Fellowship in Sri Lanka. They both supplied articulate theological and social perspectives and support for the movement. Bishop Lakshman was a founding member of CWF in 1958; Bishop Leo associated himself with its activities from the 1960s. The deaths of these leaders in 1982 and 1983 was a serious loss to CWF.

Concerned Buddhist and noted scholar K.N. Jayatillake served as a confidant and resource to Sarvodaya president Ariyaratne during the group's early development. David J. Kalupahana, a high school classmate of Ariyaratne and now a leading Buddhist philosopher, visits with him frequently when he is in Sri Lanka. Ariyaratne is the only leader of the movements studied to have headed his group continuously since its beginning. His own charismatic leadership and national prominence, together with his long service give him somewhat the character of a religious leader. Sulak of ACFOD in his writings and speeches frequently addresses Buddhist issues. However, he views his coordinator's position as a rotating one, as it has indeed been. In Thailand he often consults with monk-scholars Rajavaramuni and Buddhatat. Buddhatat is a religious and intellectual inspiration to both ACFOD and TICD. His remarkable ecumenical spirit is an important religious and intellectual resource to the Thai monks of both these movements. How much impact his teachings have at the local level of ACFOD's work is uncertain. In the case of TICD, a smaller, more cohesive, and largely student-age group, Buddhatat's work has deeply influenced its world view.

We began by observing that the sixties and the seventies evidenced a variety of movements concerned for social and economic justice. All four movements studied have been constant in their searching criticisms of the existing socioeconomic order and of the controlling groups and have experimented with a variety of programs for social change. Thus, in Karl Mannheim's terms, they are utopian. Two observations can be made to indicate some problems in keeping this "creative tension" with society. First, all four groups have engaged in practical grass-roots projects in economic self-help and community development. In fact, such projects have been Sarvodaya's major emphasis. Success at the grass-roots may lead to diminished efforts at comprehensive social and political criticism. Indeed Sarvodaya's great success at the village level seems to have shifted the sharp focus of its basic social criticisms. Certainly it is crucial to the effectiveness of the four movements studied to keep some balance between local needs, village developments, and larger prophetic judgements.

The Christian Workers Fellowship has established two centers that engage in very practical economic development programs. But ACFOD and TICD, while emphasizing grass-roots activities, do not work out of centers of their own but through local Buddhist wats, community groups, workers' and farmers' organizations, and experimental training programs. All these development programs take enormous energy, skill, and funds. They are not intended as ends in themselves but as educational avenues to a new social order. When they succeed in enhancing the local economy (like the CWF milk cooperative in Galaha or the villages where Sarvodaya has helped cultivate new land), there is always the possibility of simply building on success and neglecting the more basic social criticisms. This is part of the dialectic of "acting locally and thinking globally," and keeping the two in balance is part of the dynamics of these movements.

Second, it is quite dramatic that in the brief history of these movements, striving for economic justice and community development has involved the movements and their leaders in a broad range of conflicts, -both political and social. They have been perceived as threats to the power structure of their societies. Leaders of CWF and ACFOD have been jailed for short periods; Sarvodaya had to call off its peace march at the insistence of the prime minister. All of the movements are inherent parts of the complex strains and conflicts of their own societies. Their agendas have had to be enlarged to deal with civil rights, racial and ethnic tensions, and political instability. This expansion puts tremendous pressure on the creativity and stamina of the leaders of the movements and make the prospect of a new social order more remote. Sarvodaya hopes to build its own network of self-reliant villages into a new power structure of the nation. In Thailand there is no political party or effective alternative to challenge the shifting military cliques that have maintained their dominance in the last several years. The achievements and staying power of the movements we have studied is remarkable. Their work toward a new social order to liberate their people from poverty and oppression goes on. We cannot yet see the outcome.

Robert Bobilin, University of Hawaii

Religion and Development in Thailand

The ideological spectrum in Thai society

Orientation / Religions	Primarily Project Oriented: Unaware of (and/or uncritical of) present trends in national development	Polarized: Right	Polarized: Left	Project and Movement Oriented: Critical about present trends
Buddhists	Dhammacarik Dhammatud WFB Santi Asoke (A conservative reform movement)	Buddhatat	ACFOD CGRS TICD	Alienated students and community workers
Christians	CCT Private schools and colleges	YMCA (Chiang Mai)	CCTD	Alienated former clergy
Muslims				
No Religion			Marxists-TCP	

ACFOD - Asian Cultural Forum on Development
CCTD - Catholic Commission on Thai Development
CCT - Christian Church of Thailand
CGRS - Coordinating Group for Religion & Society
TICD - Thai Interreligious Committee for Development
WFB - World Fellowship of Buddhists

Aloysius Piersis, S.J.

Church and Development in Sri Lanka's Multi-Religious Context

(Sedec Seminar, Wennapppuwa, Jan. 27-30, 1981)

Development
The Ideological Spectrum Cutting across a Multi-Religious Society

Orientation	Primarily FOOD Oriented	FOOD & VALUE oriented	
	UNAWARE of (and/or unopposed to) present trends in development	UNEASY about the present trends	
		Polarized	
Religions		Right	Left
Buddhists		ACBC YMBA WFB	SLBM (philo Russian)
	scattered sramadana groups, Sahanadhara, samithis, etc.	(English speaking, Westernized elite	
		"Sarana" YWBA & its small projects	
		Sarvodaya	
			VDK
Hindus			
Christians	V de P Society, etc.	Private Schools, etc.	CWF Devasarana CSR Satyodaya
		Sedec	
		YMCA & NCC projects	
Muslims			
no religion			Marxists

ACBC - All Ceylon Buddhist Congress
WFB (SL) - World Fellowship of Buddhists (Sri Lanka)
SLBM - Sri Lanka Bauddha Mandalaya
VDK - Vimukti Dharma Kendraya

CWF - Christian Workers Fellowship
CSR - Centre for Society & Religion
V de P Society - Vincent de Paul Society
NCC - National Christian Council

NOTES

CHAPTER I

(1) Karl Mannheim, Essays on the Sociology of Culture, London: Routlege and Kegan Paul, 1956, p. 176.
(2) Karl Mannheim, Ideology and Utopia, New York, Harcourt, Brace and Company, 1936, p. 199.
(3) Robert N. Bellah, Religion and Progress in Modern Asia, New York, The Free Press, 1965, pp. 193-194.
(4) Barrington Moore, Jr., Injustice: The Social Bases of Obedience and Revolt, White Plains, N.Y., M. E. Sharpe, 1978, p. 482.
(5) Denis Goulet, The Cruel Choice: A New Concept in the Theory of Development, New York, Atheneum, 1977, Chapter VI.
(6) Goulet, op. cit., pp. 130-134.
(7) James C. Scott, The Moral Economy of the Peasant: Rebellion and Subsistence in Southeast Asia, New Haven, Yale University Press, 1976, p. 188.
(8) Peasant Theology, Asian Cultural Forum on Development, Bangkok, 1979, p. 4.
(9) Barrington Moore Jr., op. cit., p. 508-fin.
(10) Charles F. Keyes, "Economic Action and Buddhist Morality in a Thai Village," Journal of Asian Studies, Vol. XLII, No. 4, August 1983, p. 865.

CHAPTER II

(1) S.J. Tambiah, Spirit Cults in Northeast Thailand, Cambridge, At the University Press, 1970, p. 67.
(2) Tissa Balasuriya, The Eucharist and Human Liberation, New York, Orbis Books, 1979, p. 10.
(3) S. J. Tambiah, World Conqueror and World Renouncer: A Study of Buddhism and Polity in Thailand Against a Historical Background, New York, Cambridge University Press, 1976, p. 213.
(4) S. J. Tambiah, Ibid.
(5) Walter Vella reports that by 1830 there were ten Protestant missionaries and in 1849 there was

a Catholic Bishop, eight European priests an some nuns. See Walter F. Vella, Siam Under Rama III, 1824-1851. New York: J. J. Agustia, Inc. Monographs of the Association for Asian Studies IV. pp. 35-36.

(6) World Bank/FAO Farms Study, April 1976, as cited in Far Eastern Economic Review, July 13, 1979, p. 52.

(7) Thailand in the 1980's, The Thai University Research Association, Bangkok, 1981, p. 12.

(8) G.I.O.M. Kurukulasuriya, "Poverty in Sri Lanka," Marga, Marga Institute, February 1980, Vol. V, No. 4, pp. 21-22.

(9) Thailand in the 1980's, op. cit., pp. 10-12, and Dossier No. 17, Centre for Society and Religion, Colombo, October 1980, pp. 6-7.

(10) Godfrey Gunatilleke, "Reducing Poverty and Inequality in Sri Lanka," Dossier No. 72, Centre for Society and Religion, Colombo, October 1980, pp. 50-51. See also Charles F. Keyes, Isan: Regionalism in Northeast Thailand, Cornell Thailand Project, Interim Report Series #10, Data Paper No. 65.

(11) See U.S. Foreign Policy and the Third World, Aganda 1982. Overseas Development Council, Praeger Special Studies, N.Y., 1982, pp. 160 ff, and Day After Tomorrow in the Pacific Region, 1982, A Worldview Symposium in Cooperation with the Asia Society in Worldview, February 1982, Volume 25, Number 2, pp. 11-31. Discussions with Godfrey Gunatilleke, Marga Institute, April 1982 and lecture by Mehdi Krongkaew, Thammasat University, June 1983.

(12) Gunnar Myrdal, The Challenge of World Poverty, N.Y., Pantheon Books, 1970, p. 50.

(13) Ibid.

(14) Dossier #72, Center for Society and Religion, Colombo, October 1980, pp. 7-13 "The Thai Economic Structure," Krerkkiat Pipatseritham, Mimeographed Lecture, undated.

(15) David Morrell and Chaianaran Samudoruya, Political Conflict in Thailand, Cambridge, MA, Cum and Hain, 1981, pp. 246-249.

(16) Donald Smith, South Asian Politics and Religion, Princeton, Princeton University Press, 1966, p. 477.

(17) Joel S. Migdal, Peasants, Politics and Revolution, Princeton, Princeton University Press, 1974, p. 4-5.

CHAPTER III

(1) A. T. Ariyaratne, Collected Works, Vol. 1, Sarvodaya Research Institute, undated, p. 48.
(2) A. T. Ariyaratne, Collected Works, Volume II, Sarvodaya Research Institute, Colombo, 1980, pp. 96-97.
(3) A. T. Ariyaratne, Sarvodaya and Development, Moratuwa, Sri Lanka, Sarvodaya Publication, 1980, p.5.
(4) A. T. Ariyaratne, Collected Works, Vol. II, Colombo, Sarvodaya Research Institute, 1980, p. 32.
(5) Ibid.
(6) A. T. Ariyaratne, Collected Works, Colombo, Sarvodaya Research Institute, 1980, pp. 131-132.
(7) Ariyaratne, op. cit., pp. 132-133.
(8) Joanna Macy, Dharma and Development: Religion as Resource in the Sarvodaya Self-Help Movement, West Hartford, CT, Kumarian Press, 1983, p. 29.
(9) Interview, May 1982.
(10) Ten Basic Human Needs and Their Satisfaction, Sarvodaya Development Education Institute, Moratuwa, Sri Lanka, 1981.
(11) Ibid.
(12) Nandasena Ratnapala, Study Service in Sarvodaya, Colombo, Sarvodaya Research Center, 1977, p. 111.
(13) Joanna Macy, Dharma and Development, West Hartford, CT, Kumarian Press, 1983, pp. 66-69.
(14) Lanka Tathika Sarvodaya Shramadana Sangamaya, Annual Service Report, 1981, Moratuwa, Sri Lanka, Sarvodaya Research Institute, pp. 52-53 and Study Service in Sarvodaya, op. cit., pp. 68-72.
(15) Denis Goulet, Survival with Integrity: Sarvodaya at the Crossroads, Colombo, Sri Lanka: Marga Institute, 1981, p. 96, ftn. 38.
(16) A.T. Ariyaratne, Collected Works, Vol. 1, Columbo Sarvodaya Research Institute, 1982, pp. 140-141.
(17) Interview, May 1982.
(18) Joanna Macy, op. cit., p. 87.
(19) Ibid..
(20) Clifford Geertz, Old Societies and New States: The Quest for Modernity in Asia and Africa, New York, 1963, pp. 103-157.

CHAPTER IV

(1) G.J. Lenski, Origins of Trotskyism in Ceylon, Stanford: Hoover Institution, 1968, pp. 22-28.
(2) Facing the Future: Meeting the Crisis, Christian Workers Fellowship, Colombo, March 1975, p. 4.
(3) The Christian Worker and the Trade Union, Christian Workers Fellowship, Colombo, November 1958, 2nd (revised) reprint, January 1976, p. 6.
(4) Christian Worker, Bulletin of the Christian Workers Fellowship, Colombo, 1981, Third Quarter, pp. 26-27.
(5) "The Sacrament of Repentance," Christian Workers Fellowship, Colombo, mimeographed, undated, p. 6.
(6) "Agape Service," Christian Workers Fellowship, Colombo, undated, p. 2.
(7) The Worker's Mass, Christian Workers Fellowship, Colombo, 1982.
(8) Letter from Vijaya Vidvasagara, for the Christian Worker, March 20, 1985.
(9) Lanka Guardian, July 15, 1979, Vol. 2, No. 6, "Book Review" section.
(10) Facing the Future: Meeting the Crisis, Christian Workers Fellowship, Colombo, March, 1975, "Introductory Note".
(11) op. cit., p. 4.
(12) Nawaz Dawood; Tea and Poverty, 1980, Kowloon, Hong Kong, Urban Rural Mission--Christian Mission of Asia, pp. 44-45.
(13) For the Dawning of the New, Jeffrey Abayasekera and Dr. Preman Niles, ed., Christian Conference of Asia, Singapore, 1981.
(14) For the Dawning of the New Day, Jeffrey Abayasekera and Dr. Preman Niles, ed., Christian Conference of Asia, Singapore, 1981, p. 42.
(15) Christian Workers Fellowship, Rural Perspectives, Colombo, June 1981, pp. 4-6.
(16) Excerpt from speech by Bishop Wickremesinghe in Living in Christ with People, Niles Memorial Lecture Christian Conference of Asia, Bangalore, India, 1981, as reprinted in Christian Worker, fourth quarter, 1983, p. 17.

CHAPTER V

(1) S. J. Tambiah, World Conqueror and World Renouncer, Cambridge, Cambridge University Press, 1976, pp. 254-255.

(2) See Puey Ungphakorn, A Siamese for All Seasons, Bangkok Komal Keemthong Foundation, 1981, pp. 70-93. Also David Morell and Chai-anan Samudavanija, Political Conflict in Thailand, Cambridge, Massachusetts, Oelgeschager, Gunn and Hain, 1981.

(3) Thai Inter Religious Commission for Development, Section on "Activities and Work Plans", 1981-1982, Bangkok, Thailand.

(4) Ibid.

(5) S. J. Tambiah, Dialectic in Practical Religion, Cambridge Papers in Social Anthropology 5, ed. E. R. Leader, Cambridge University Press, pp. 41-122.

(6) Jane Bunnag, Buddhist Monk and Buddhist Layman: A Study of Urban Monastic Organization in Central Thailand, Cambridge, Cambridge University Press, 1973, pp. 43-50.

(7) Interviews in Bangkok in Spring 1982.

(8) Aphichat Chamratrithirang, et. al., Recent Migrants in Bangkok Metropolis: A Follow-up Study of Migrant's Adjustment, Assimilation and Integration, Institute for Population and Social Research, Mahidol University, Bangkok, November, 1979, pp. 76-79.

(9) Environmental Study of Bangkok, Bangkok, Geography Department, Chulalongkorn University, 1981.

(10) Jane Bunnag; op. cit., p. 145.

(11) Samenera Training School, Thai Interreligious Commission on Development, Bangkok, 1981.

(12) Toward the Truth, Buddhadasa, Edited by Donald K. Swearer, Philadelphia Westiminster Press, 1971.

(13) Donald K. Swearer; Buddhism in Transition, Philadelphia Westminster Press, 1970. Also "is Asian Religion World Rejecting?", Donald Swearer, 1977, Schaff Lectures, Pittsubrg Theological Seminary, Unpublished Manuscript.

(14) Donald K. Swearer, "Bhikkhu Buddhadasa on Ethics and Society", 1981, Unpublished Manuscript.

(15) Buddhadasa-bhikkhu, No Religion, Translated from the Thai bay Bhikkhu Punno, Sublime Life Mission, Bangkok, 1975, p. 11.

(16) e.g., Dharma: The World Saviour, pp. 23-24, and No Religion, pp. 88-89.
(17) Christianity and Buddhism, p. 30.
(18) op. cit., p. 31.
(19) op. cit., p. 26.
(20) op. cit., p. 29.
(21) op. cit., p. 34.
(22) op. cit., p. 3.
(23) op. cit., p. 38.
(24) op. cit., p. 94.
(25) op. cit., p. 111.
(26) Dharma: The World Saviour, Bangkok, 2512, pp. 34-36.
(27) No Religion, Swearer, p. 102.
(28) Interview, February 1982.
(29) "Exchanging Dharma While Fighting", Visakha Puja, Bangkok, May 1970, p. 42.
(30) op. cit., p. 45.
(31) Visakha Puja, op. cit., p. 33.
(32) Interview in Spring 1982. See also Swearer, Donald; "Bhikkhu Buddhasa on Ethics and Society", op. cit., p. 10.
(33) Donald K. Swearer, "Bhikkhu Buddhasa on Ethics and Society", op. cit., p. 11.

CHAPTER VI

(1) Asian Cultural Forum on Development, Constitution, June 1979, p. 2.
(2) Sulak Sivaraksa, A Buddhist Vision for Renewing Society, Bangkok, Thai Watana, 1981, p. 67.
(3) A Buddhist Vision for Renewing Society, p. 187.
(4) Asian Action Newsletter of the Asian Cultural Forum on Development, No. 1, January 1976, p. 2.
(5) Ibid.
(6) "ACT Highlights", Asian Action, No. 11, November-February 1977, p. 15.
(7) People's Action in Asia, Report of the Joint ACFOD-FAO/AP Workshop and First ACFOD Council, Bangkok, Thailand, June 1977, p. 20.
(8) op. cit., pp. 26-28.
(9) Asian Action; Newsletter of the Asian Cultural Forum on Development, No. 4, May-June, 1976, p. 2.

(10) Sulak Sivaraksa, "Religion and Development," in Nancy Ing, Editor, Questioning Development in Southeast Asia, Singapore, Select Books, 1977, p. 18.
(11) Human Resource Development in Asia: A Report of ACFOD's Development Workers' Programme, 1977, Bangkok, Thailand.
(12) Report on Trainers Training Program I, May 20 to June 25, 1981, Asian Forum on Cultural Development, ACFOD, Bangkok.
(13) Asian Action, Newsletter of the Asian Forum for Cultural Development, Bangkok, No. 19, 1979.
(14) As reported by Keith Warren, Asian Action, No. 4, May-June 1976.

CHAPTER VII

(1) Sulak Sivaraksa, Letter, December 1, 1984.
(2) Ibid.
(3) Bardwell L. Smith, editor, Religion and Legitimation of Power in Sri Lanka, Cambersburg, Pennsylvania, Anima Books, 1978, p. 80.
(4) S.P. Amarasingam, "The Ethnic Problems and the Socio-Political Situation in Sri Lanka Today", unpublished manuscript of paper presented to the Sri Lanka Foundation Institute, September 4, 1984.
(5) Tissa Balasuriya, "Catastrophe, July '83: Can Sri Lanka Survive," Logos, Volume 22 No. 4, December 1983, p. 33.
(6) Sarvodaya Office, People's Declaration for National Peace and Harmony, Morutawa, Sri Lanka, October 1983, p. 13.
(7) Sarvodaya Office, op. cit., p. 21.
(8) Nandasena Ratnapala, Study Service in Sarvodaya, Colombo, Sarvodaya Research Center, 1977, p. 76.
(9) Joanna Macy, op. cit., pp. 29-30.
(10) S. Pamarasingam, op. cit., p. 18.
(11) Sarvodaya Office, People's Declaration for National Peace and Harmony, op. cit., p. 25.
(12) Christian Worker, Colombo, Third Quarter, 1984, p. 7.
(13) Christian Worker, op. cit., p. 4.
(14) A. T. Ariyaratne, Collected Works, Vol. I, op.cit., p. 132.
(15) S. J. Tambiah, Buddhism and the Spirit Cults in Northeast Thailand, op.cit., pp. 64-65.

(16) Sulak Sivaraksa, Siamese Resurgence, Bangkok, Asian Cultural Forum on Development, 1985, p. 107.

(17) Joanna Macy, op.cit., p. 45.

BIBLIOGRAPHY

Ariyaratne, A.T. *A Struggle to Awaken.* Moratuwa, Sri Lanka: Sarvodaya Press, 1978.

_______________. *Collected Works,* Vol. I & II, Dehiwale, Sri Lanka: Sarvodaya Research Institute, 1980.

_______________. *In Search of Development: Sarvodaya Effort to Harmonize Tradition with Change*. Moratuwa, Sri Lanka: Sarvodaya Press, 1982.

Bellah, Robert. *Religion and Progress in Modern Asia*. New York: The Free Press, 1965.

_______________. *Beyond Belief: Essays on Religion in a Post-Traditional World*. New York: Harper & Row, 1970.

Balasuriya, Tissa. *The Eucharist and Human Liberation*. New York: Orbis Press, 1979.

Buddadasabhikkhu. *Another Kind of Birth*. Bangkok, Thailand: Sublime Life Mission, undated.

_______________. *Christianity and Buddhism*. Bangkok, Thailand: Sublime Life Mission, 1967(?).

_______________. *Dhamma: The World Saviour*. Bangkok, Thailand: Sublime Life Mission, undated.

_______________. No Religion. Bangkok, Thailand: Sublime Life Mission, undated.

_______________. *Two Kinds of Language*. Bangkok, Thailand: Sublime Life Mission, undated.

_______________. *Why Were We Born?*. Bangkok, Thailand: Sublime Life Mission, undated.

Bunnag, Jane. *Buddhist Monk, Buddhist Laymen: A Study of Urban Monastic Organization in Central Thailand*. Cambridge, England: Cambridge University Press, 1973.

Carter, John Ross. *Religiousness in Sri Lanka*. Colombo, Sri Lanka: Marga Institute, 1979.

Ching, Nancy, ed. Questioning Development in Southeast Asia. Singapore: Select Books on Behalf of Southeast Asia Study Group, 1977.

Dawood, Nawaz. Tea and Poverty. Hong Kong: Urban Rural Mission, Christian Conference of Asia, 1980.

Eisenstadt, S.N. Modernization, Protest and Change. Englewood Cliffs: Prentice-Hall, 1966.

Evers, Hans-Dieter, ed. Modernization in Southeast Asia. Singapore: Oxford University Press, 1975.

Geertz, Clifford, ed. Old Societies and New States: The Quest for Modernity in Asia and Africa. New York: Free Press, 1963.

_______________, The Interpretation of Cultures. New York: Basic Books, 1973.

Goulet, Denis. Survival with Integrity: Sarvodaya at the Crossroads. Colombo, Sri Lanka: Marga Institute, 1981.

_____________. The Cruel Choice, A New Concept in the Theory of Development. New York: Atheneum Press, 1971.

Girling, John L.S. Thailand: Society and Politics. Ithaca, N.Y.: Cornell University Press, 1981.

Goldthrorpe, J.E. The Sociology of the Third World: Disparity and Involvement. New York: Cambridge University Press, 1975.

Gombrich, Richard F. Precept and Practice: Traditional Buddhism in the Rural Highlands of Ceylon. London: Oxford University Press, 1971.

Cunatilleke, Godfrey; Tiruchelvan, Neelan; Commaraswamy, Radhika. Ethical Dilemmas of Development in Asia. Lexington, Massachusetts: Lexington Books, 1983.

_______________. "Participatory Development and Dependence--the Case of Sri Lanka", Marga Quarterly Journal, Special Issue Vol. 5 No. 3 , Colombo, Sri Lanka: Marga Institute, 1978.

_______________. Welfare and Growth in Sri Lanka. Marga Research Studies--No. 2., Colombo, Sri Lanka: Marga Institute, 1974.

___________, ed. Religion and Development in Asian Societies. Colombo, Sri Lanka, 1974.

Hainsworth, Geoffrey B. Village-Level Modernization in Southeast Asia: The Political Economy of Rice and Water. Vancouver, British Columbia: University of British Columbia Press, 1982.

Houtart, Francois. Religion and Ideology in Sri Lanka. Maryknoll, N.Y.: Orbis Press, 1974.

Hughes, Philip J. Thai Culture, Values, and Religion. Chaing Mai, Thailand Manuscript Division, Payap College, 1981.

Ishii, Yoneo. "A Note on Buddhistic Millenarian Revolts in Northeastern Siam", Journal of Southeast Asian Studies, 1975, 15:90-101.

Karunatilake, H.N.S. This Confused Society. Colombo, Sri Lanka: Buddhist Information Centre, 1976.

Keyes, Charles F. "Millenialism, Theravada Buddhism, and Thai Society." Journal of Asian Studies, 36:2, February 1977, pp. 283-302.

_______________. "Economic Action and Buddhist Morality in a Thai Village." Journal of Asian Studies, 42:2, August 1983.

Kurukulasuriya, G.I.O.M. "Poverty in Sri Lanka", Marga Quarterly Journal, Marga Institute, Colombo, Sri Lanka, Vol. 5 No. 4 , 1978 and Vol. 6 No. 1, 1980.

Lenski, G.J. Origins of Trotskyism in Ceylon. Stanford: Hoover Institution, 1968.

Lewy, Guenter. Religion and Revolution. New York: Oxford University Press, 1974.

Macy, Joanna. Dharma and Development: Religion as a Resource in the Sarvodaya Self-Help Movement. West Hartford, Connecticut: Kumarian Press, 1983.

Mannheim, Karl. Ideology and Utopia. New York: Harcourt, Brace, and Company, 1975.

Moore, Barrington, Jr. Social Origins of Dictatorship and Decomocracy. Boston: Beacon Press, 1966.

________________. Injustice: The Social Bases of Obedience and Revolt. White Plains, N.Y.: M.E. Sharpe, 1978.

Morell, David; Chai-anan, Samudavanija. Political Conflict in Thailand: Reform, Reaction, Revolution. Cambridge, Massachusetts: Oelgeschlager, Gunn and Hain, 1981.

Myrdal, Gunnar. Economic Theory and the Underdeveloped Regions. London: Duckworth, 1957.

______________. Asian Drama: An Inquiry Into the Poverty of Nations. New York: Pantheon, 1968.

Marga Institute, Religion and Development in Asian Societies. Colombo: Marga Publishing, 1974.

Nisbet, Robert A. History of the Idea of Progress. New York: Basic Books, 1980.

Olson, Grant. "Sangha Reform in Thailand: Limitation, Liberation and the Middle Path". Master's Thesis, University of Hawaii, 1983.

Peacock, James L.; Kirsch, A. Thomas. The Human Direction. New York: Appleton-Century-Crofts, 1973.

Puey, Ungphakorm. Best Wishes for Asia. Bangkok: Klett Thai Publications, 1975.

______________. A Siamese for All Seasons. Bangkok: Komol Keemthong Foundation, 1981.

Popkin, Samuel L. The Rational Peasant: The Political Economy of Rural Society in Vietnam. Berkeley and Los Angeles: University of California Press, 1979.

Rahula, Walpola. The Heritage of the Bhikku. New York: Grove Press, 1974.

Roberts, Michael, ed. Collective Identities and Protest in Modern Sri Lanka. Colombo, Sri Lanka: Marga Institute, 1979.

Scott, James C. The Moral Economy of the Peasant. New Haven: Yale University Press, 1976.

Siddhi Butr-Indr. The Social Philosophy of Buddhism. Bangkok: Mahamakut Buddhist University, 1973.

Smith, Bardwell, ed. Religion and Legitimation of Power in Thailand, Laos, and Burma. Cambersburg, Pennsylvania: Anima Press, 1978.

___________________. Religion and Legitimation of Power in Sri Lanka. Cambersburgh, Pennsylvania: Anima Press, 1978.

Somboon Suksamran. Political Buddhism in Southeast Asia. London: C. Hurst & Co., 1977.

Soedjatmoko, Development and Freedom. Tokyo, Japan: The Simul Press, 1980.

Sivaraksa, Sulak. Siam in Crisis. Bangkok: Komol Keemthong Foundation, 1970.

___________________. Siamese Resurgence. Bangkok Asian Cultural Forum on Development, 1985.

___________________. A Buddhist Vision for Renewing Society. Bangkok: Thai Watana Panich, 1981.

Smith, Donald. South Asian Politics and Religion. Princeton, New Jersey: Princeton University Press, 1966.

___________________. Religion, Politics and Social Change in the Third World. New York: The Free Press, 1971.

Swearer, Donald. Buddhism in Transition. Philadelphia: The Westminster Press, 1970.

___________________, ed. Toward the Truth: Buddhadasa. Philadelphia: The Westminster Press, 1971.

________________. Buddhism and Society in Southeast Asia. Chamberburg, Pennsylvania: Anima Press, 1981.

Tambiah, S.J. Buddhism and the Spirit Cults in Northeast Thailand. London: Cambridge University Press, 1970.

______________. World Conqueror and World Renouncer. London: Cambridge University Press, 1976.

Wijesinghe, Mallory. Sri Lanka's Development Thrust. Colombo, Sri Lanka: Aitken and Spence, 1981.

Wilson, Jeyaratnam A. Politics in Sri Lanka 1947-1973. New York: St. Martin's Press, 1974.

Wriggins, W. Howard; Guyot, James F. Population, Politics and the Future of Southern Asia. New York: Columbia University Press, 1973.

Periodicals

Asian Action. Newsletter of the Asian Cultural Forum on Development. Bi-monthly. ACFOD Secretariat, GPO Box 2930 Bangkok 10501, Thailand.

Dana. Newsletter of Sarvodaya Shramadana. Monthly. Sarvodaya Headquarters, Damsak Mandira, 98 Rawatawatt Road, Moratuwa, Sri Lanka.

Christian Worker. Quarterly of the Christian Workers Fellowship. Christian Workers Fellowship, 39, Bristol Street, Colombo 1--Sri Lanka.

Logos. Centre for Society and Religion. Four issues a year. Centre for Society and Religion, 281 Deans Road, Colombo 10, Sri Lanka.

CCPD Documents. Reports and background papers of the World Council of Churches Commission on the Churches' Participation in Development. 150, route de Ferney, 1211 Geneva 20 Switzerland.

Index